I CAN DRAW
SHARKS AND WHALES

BY GILL SPEIRS

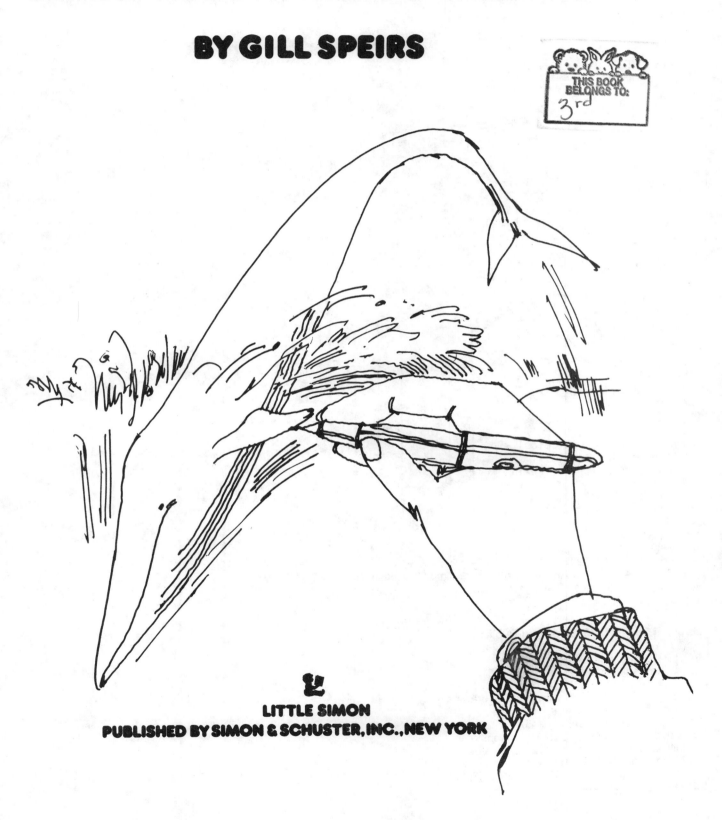

LITTLE SIMON
PUBLISHED BY SIMON & SCHUSTER, INC., NEW YORK

Published by LITTLE SIMON,
A division of Simon & Schuster, Inc.
Simon & Schuster Building
Rockefeller Center
1230 Avenue of the Americas
New York, New York 10020
LITTLE SIMON and colophon are trademarks of Simon & Schuster, Inc.
Manufactured in the United States of America
    4 5 6 7 8 9 10

Library of Congress Cataloging-in-Publication Data

Speirs, Gill.
   I can draw sharks and whales.

   Summary: Step-by-step instructions for drawing a
variety of sharks and whales in different poses.
   1. Sharks in art—Juvenile literature. 2. Whales in
art—Juvenile literature. 3. Drawing—Technique—
Juvenile literature. [1. Sharks in art. 2. Whales in
art. 3. Drawing—Technique] I. Title.
NC781.S65   1986   743'.6731   85-23135
ISBN 0-671-60477-5

HERE'S HOW

Whales and sharks are the most awesome creatures found in the oceans of the world today. Some whales are bigger than any beast ever known to have existed. Sharks have a worldwide reputation for ferocity, which in some cases is well deserved.

I CAN DRAW WHALES AND SHARKS will show you how you can learn to draw many of the different whales and sharks. The book tells you how to use basic shapes to build up their forms, and it describes the colors and markings that often distinguish one type of whale or shark from another.

Whales and sharks need to be able to move through the water with speed and ease, and their outer form is well designed for this. Apart from their fins and teeth, they have no sharp angles and their outlines are smooth and streamlined.

Before you start to follow the easy instructions in this book, practice using your pen or pencil to draw smooth, flowing lines. Read the section GETTING STARTED and try to make the different textures shown there. They will help make your drawings of whales and sharks even more exciting.

As an extra bonus, the last pages and the back cover of this book have a group of shapes that can be fitted together to form patterns of the different whales and sharks. You can use these to help you draw.

Don't feel discouraged if your first attempts at drawing a whale or shark are not quite right. Mistakes don't matter and you can always start again. Practice as often as you can and you will soon be able to draw whales and sharks just the way you want to.

GETTING STARTED

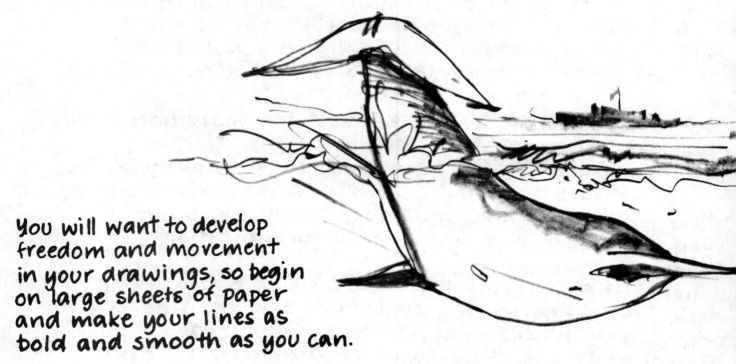

You will want to develop
freedom and movement
in your drawings, so begin
on large sheets of paper
and make your lines as
bold and smooth as you can.

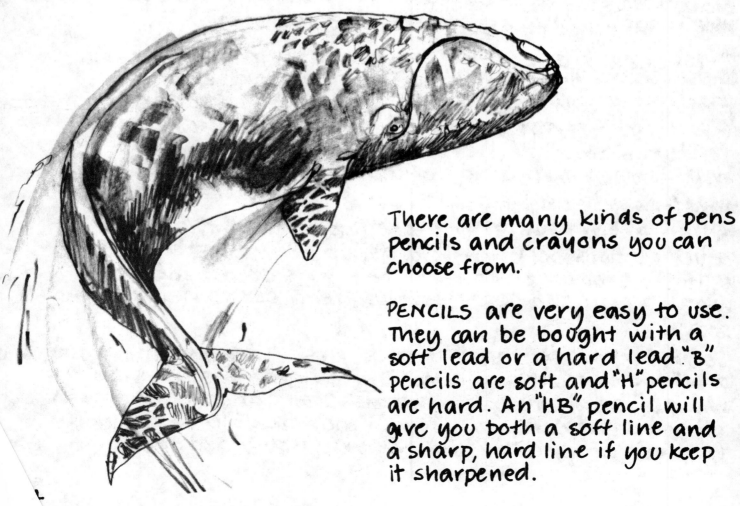

There are many kinds of pens
pencils and crayons you can
choose from.

PENCILS are very easy to use.
They can be bought with a
soft lead or a hard lead. "B"
pencils are soft and "H" pencils
are hard. An "HB" pencil will
give you both a soft line and
a sharp, hard line if you keep
it sharpened.

CHARCOAL makes a very soft, very black line. It can be bought in sticks or in a pencil, which is much cleaner and easier to use. You can smudge charcoal with your finger to make shading. But take care not to smudge by accident!

PASTELS are similar to charcoal and come in lots of colors.

PENS are available in many varieties. The cheapest and easiest to use are those with a fiber or felt tip. These can be bought with many different widths and lots of different colors.

Many other types of pens can be used for drawing. Fountain pens, mapping pens, crowquill pens and bamboo pens all give their own kinds of lines. You can wet the ink with a brush and water for delicate washes. Or you may wish to make strong contrasts with areas of very black ink.

HOW TO USE THE DIAGRAMS

The following 5 drawings show you the stages to go through when you start to learn to draw whales and sharks using the diagrams in this book.

1. Begin by drawing a curved line the length you wish your drawing to be. It should indicate the direction of the whale or shark you wish to draw.

2. Draw circles along the line to build up the shape of the body.

3 Draw a smooth outline using the edges of the circles as a guide.

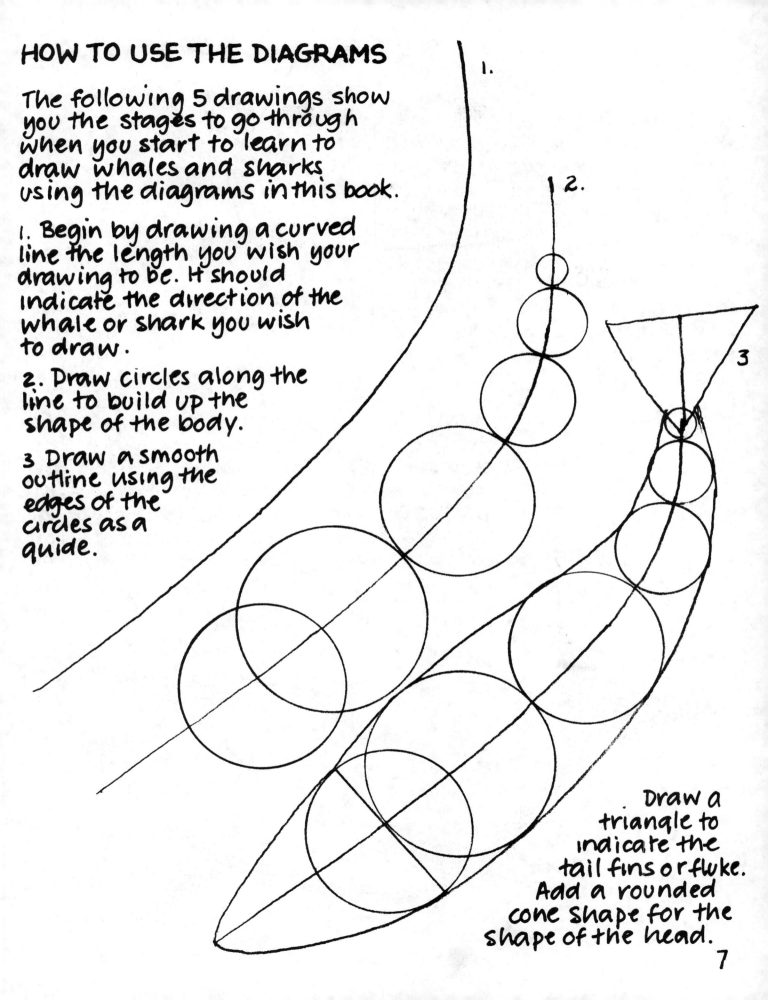

1.

2.

3

. Draw a triangle to indicate the tail fins or fluke. Add a rounded cone shape for the shape of the head.

7

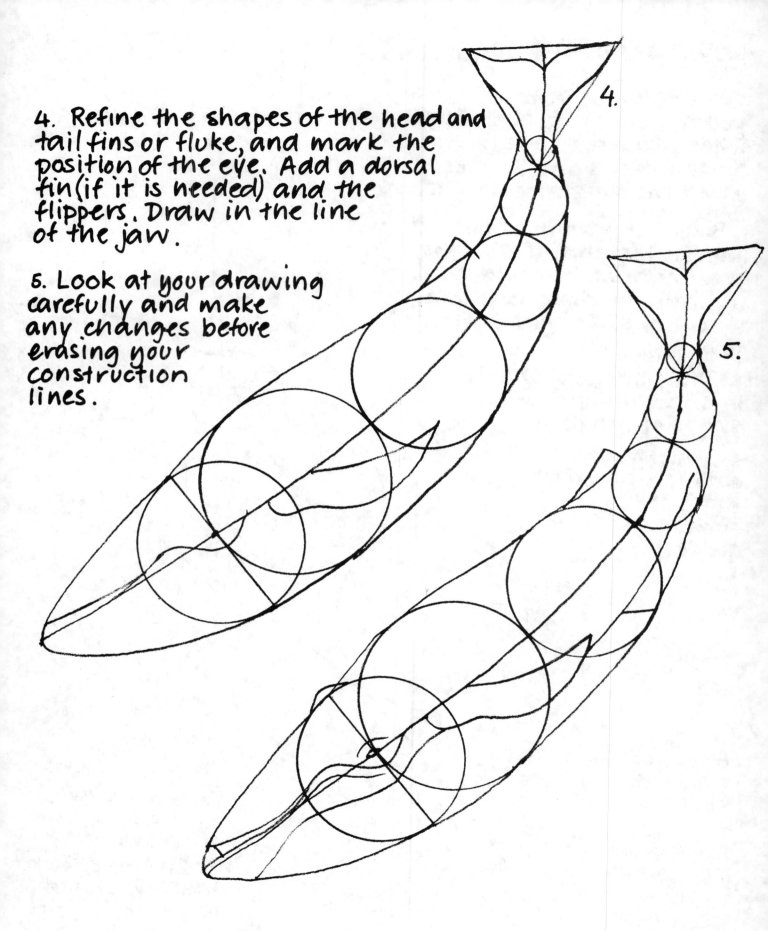

4. Refine the shapes of the head and tail fins or fluke, and mark the position of the eye. Add a dorsal fin (if it is needed) and the flippers. Draw in the line of the jaw.

5. Look at your drawing carefully and make any changes before erasing your construction lines.

8

Any details and skin textures
should be added only when
you are pleased with the
basic form of your drawing.

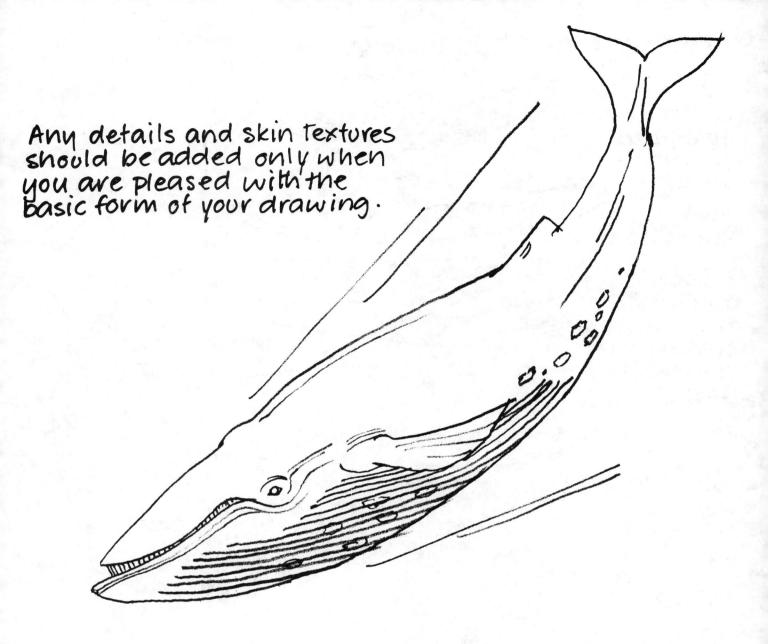

After you have practiced drawing whales and sharks this
way, you will find that you will have developed enough
skill and knowledge skip some of the stages.

Remember that each whale or shark has its own very
distinctive characteristics. Be sure to use the correct
types of fins, flippers, tail or fluke, jaw lines, and
skin textures.

COMPARATIVE SIZES OF WHALES

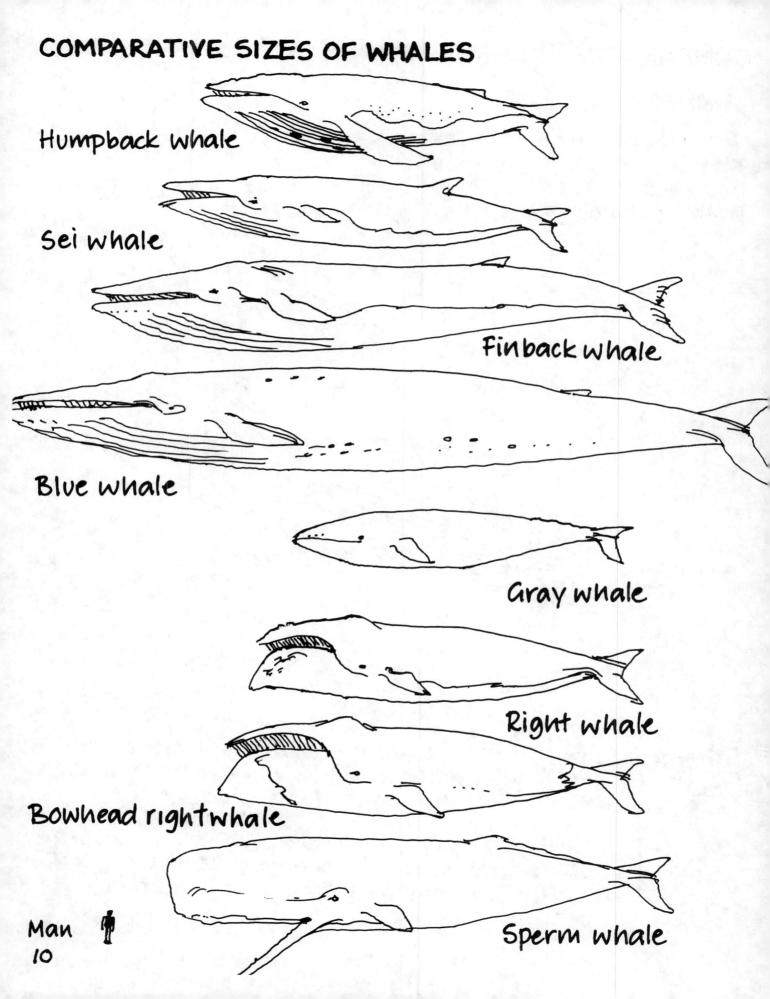

Humpback whale

Sei whale

Finback whale

Blue whale

Gray whale

Right whale

Bowhead right whale

Man

10

Sperm whale

COMPARATIVE SIZES OF SHARKS

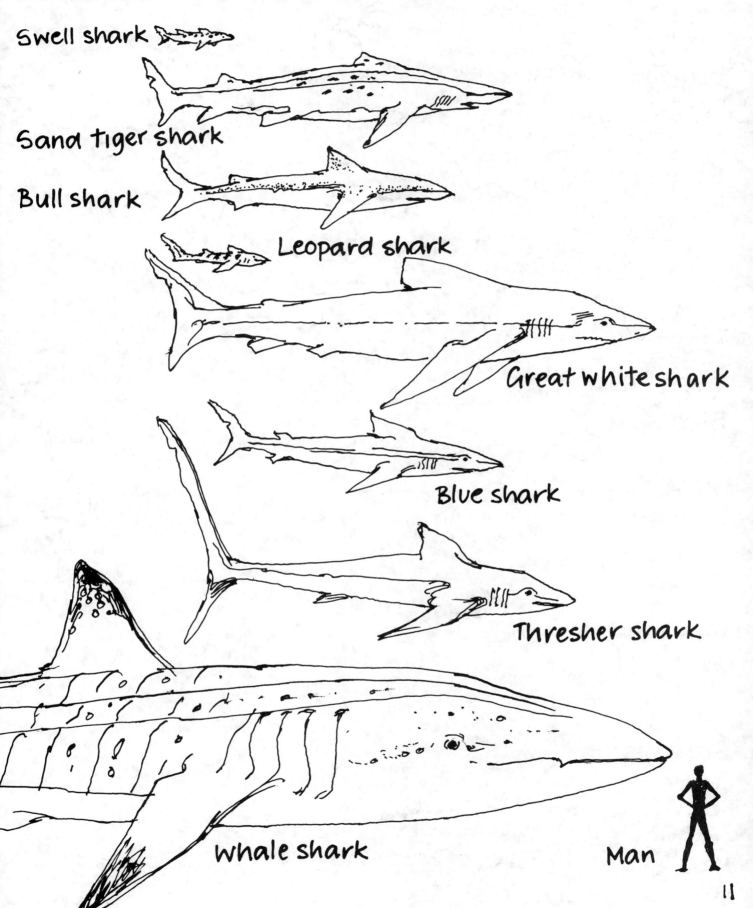

Swell shark

Sand tiger shark

Bull shark

Leopard shark

Great white shark

Blue shark

Thresher shark

whale shark

Man

11

WHERE WHALES AND SHARKS LIVE

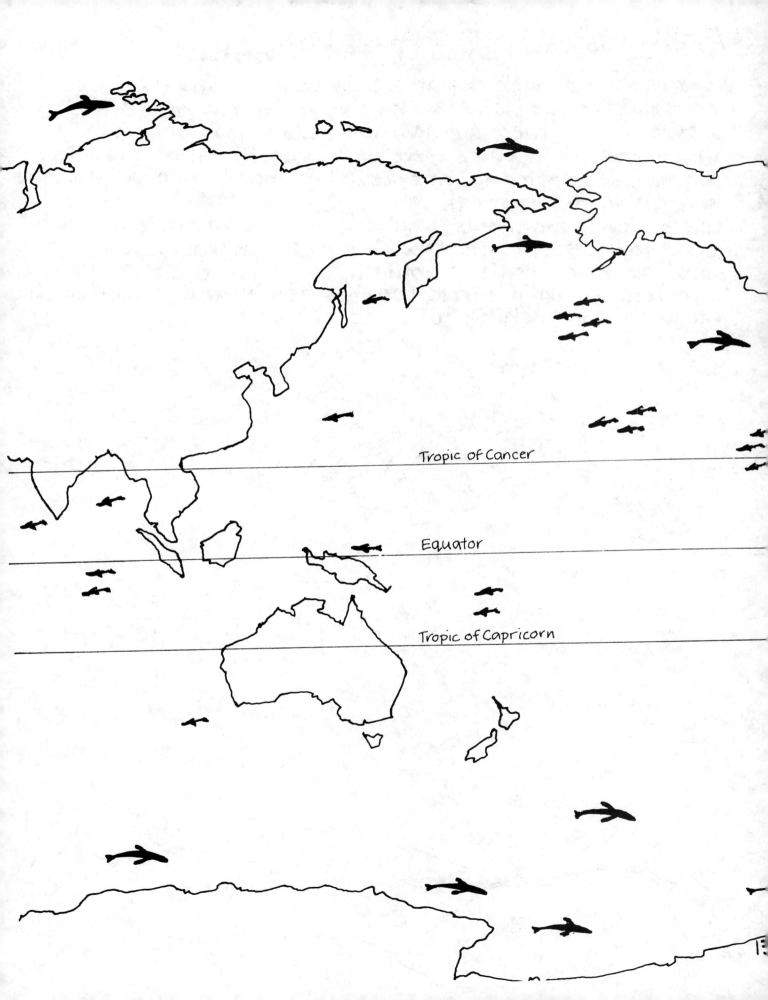

Tropic of Cancer

Equator

Tropic of Capricorn

SKELETONS AND BASIC SHAPES OF WHALES

Whales are mammals and are descendants of land-dwelling animals. The skeleton of a whale shows the remnant of a pelvic girdle. There are no traces of hind legs, but bones in the flippers show where there were once five fingers. Whales are now so adapted to their ocean life that their bone structure is not able to support them out of the water.

Like all other mammals, whales must breathe air to live. They come to the surface to take in air. The characteristic spouting of a whale is actually air being let out. This air vaporizes when it meets the outside air and it looks as if the whale is pushing out water.

A pygmy right whale

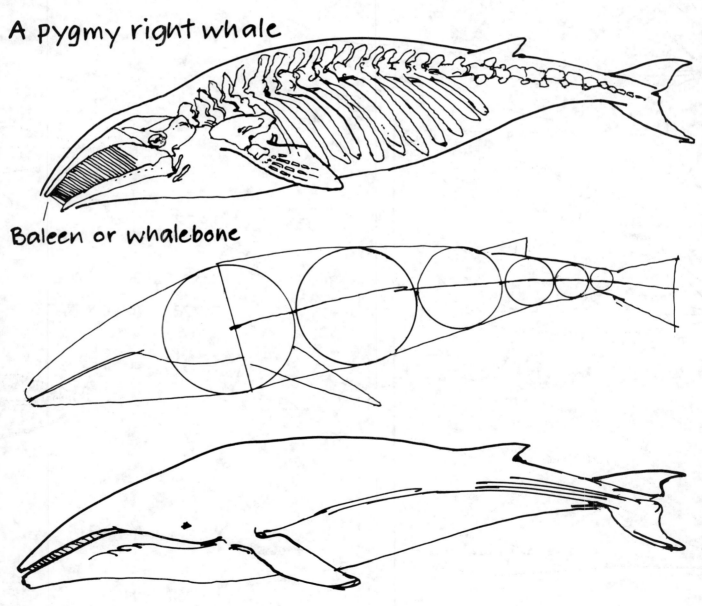

Baleen or whalebone

14

Whales belong to one or the other of two groups: baleen whales or toothed whales. The two whales shown here are baleen whales and have rows of baleen or whalebone hanging from the upper jaw This whalebone is used to sieve plankton or krill — the food on which they live — from the water.

A right whale

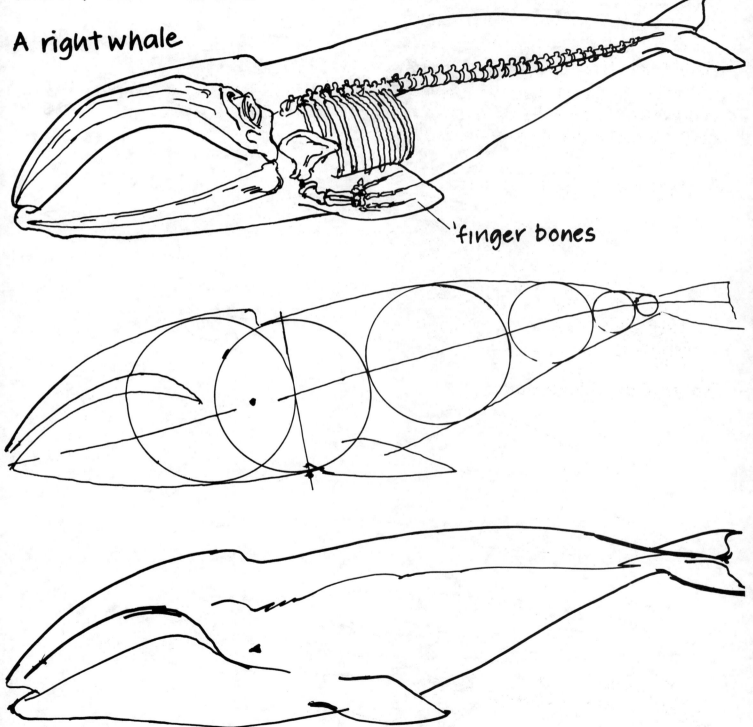

'finger bones

The tail of a whale has developed into a horizontal fluke.
This is quite different than the vertical tail fins of fish.

A humpback whale

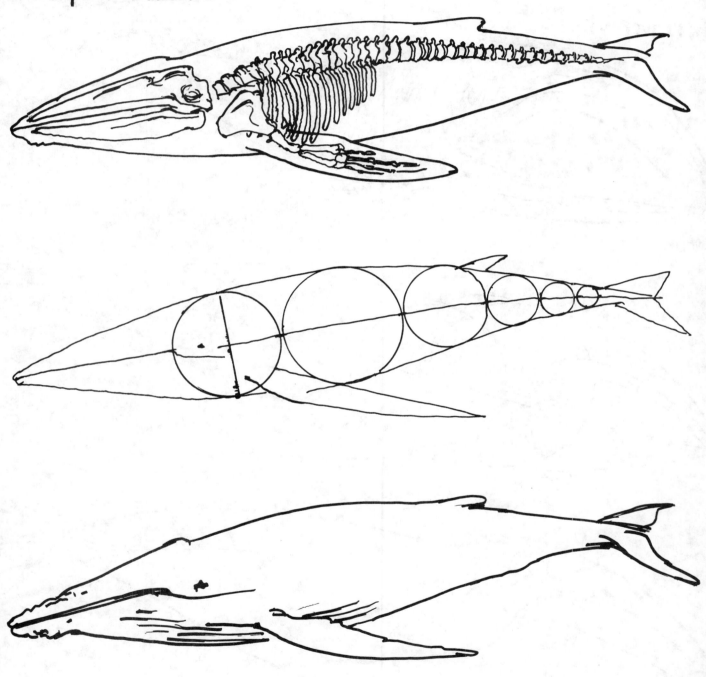

The toothed whales form a much larger group than the baleen whales. This group includes all the whales known as dolphins and porpoises. The mouth of a toothed whale usually displays teeth only on the lower jaw. These are conical and fit into sockets in the upper jaw. The number of teeth varies from a single tooth to more than 20, depending on the type of whale.

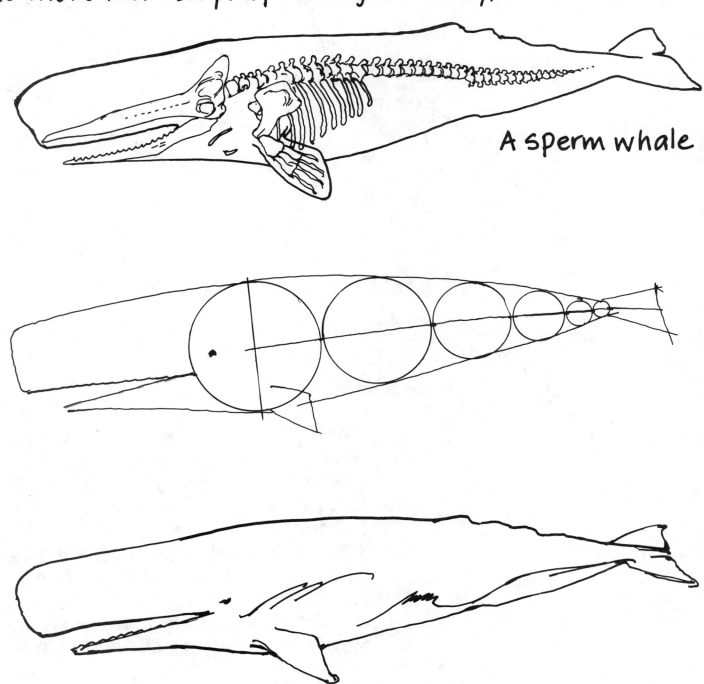

A sperm whale

SPERM WHALE (<u>Physeter catodon</u>)
All oceans of the world

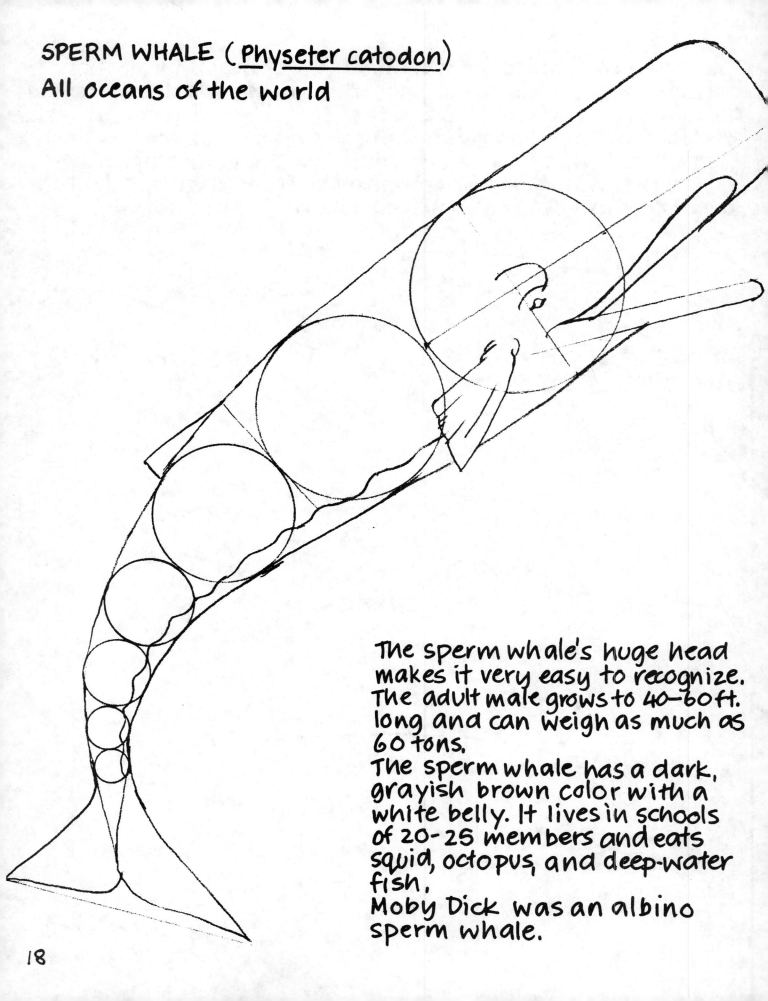

The sperm whale's huge head makes it very easy to recognize. The adult male grows to 40-60 ft. long and can weigh as much as 60 tons.
The sperm whale has a dark, grayish brown color with a white belly. It lives in schools of 20-25 members and eats squid, octopus, and deep-water fish.
Moby Dick was an albino sperm whale.

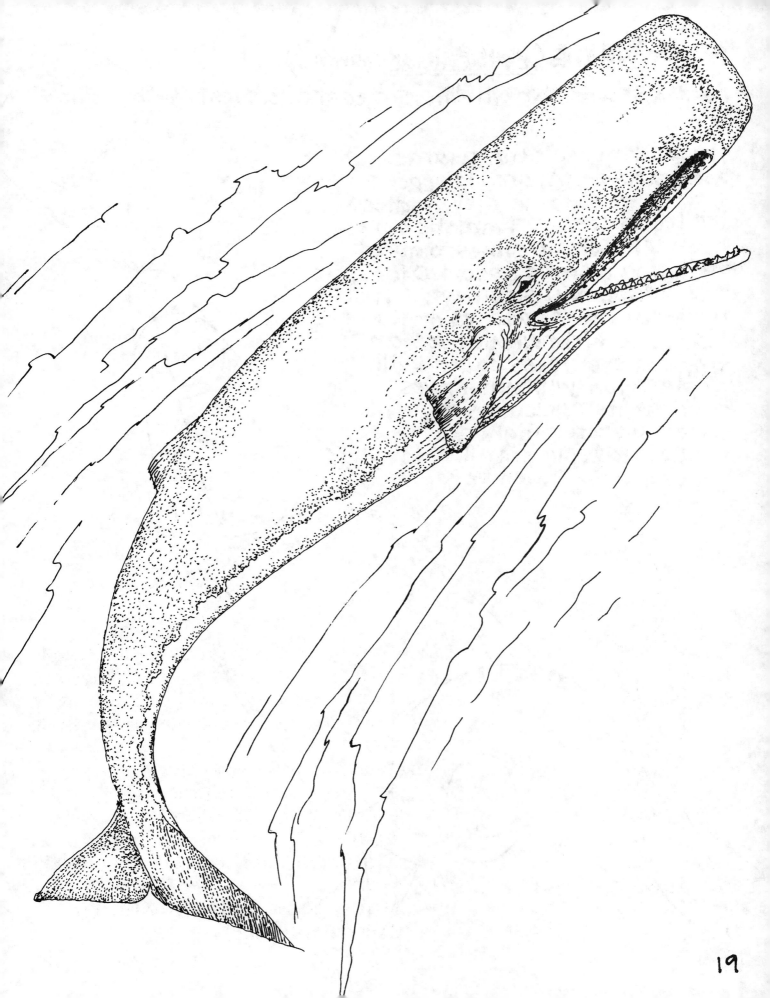

RIGHT WHALE (<u>Balaenidae</u> family)
East and west North Atlantic, east and west North Pacific

The right whale has a large head and a very arched upper jaw that contains sieve plates (called baleen or whalebone). The right whale grows to about 60 ft. and weighs up to 120 tons. It Is black or bluish gray with irregular white patches on the belly. The right whale lives on tiny sea creatures called krill or plankton, which it sieves through its baleen as it takes in water. Right whales travel in small groups of 3—8 members.

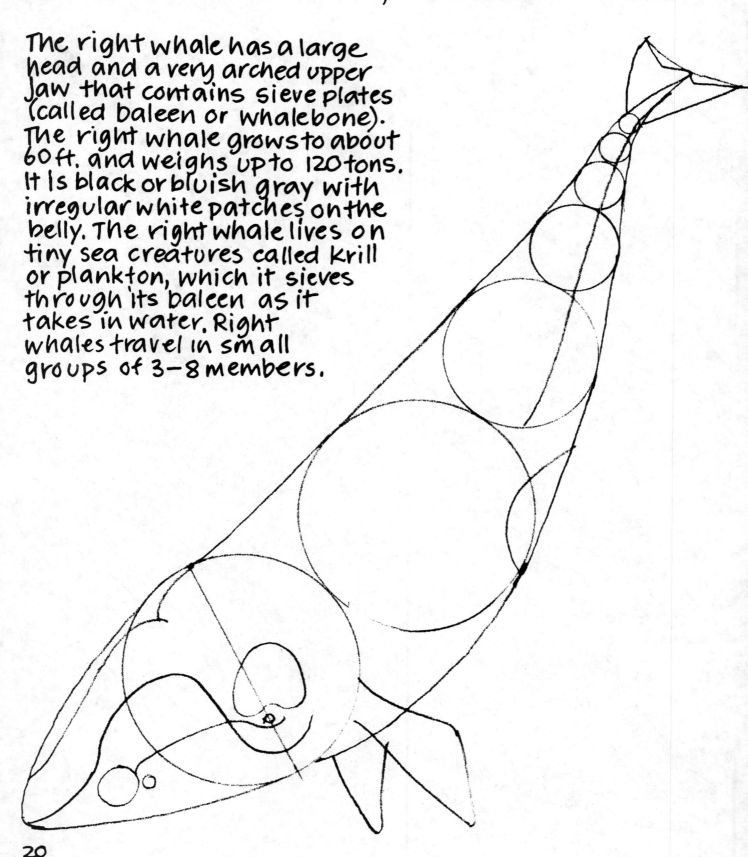

HUMPBACK WHALE (<u>Megaptera novaeangliae</u>)
Arctic and Antarctic waters

The humpback whale is a member of the baleen family. It is short and heavy, with rough skin and long flippers that are often covered with whale lice and barnacles. Humpback whales are very friendly and playful, and although they are slow they are sometimes seen leaping clear out of the water with great elegance.

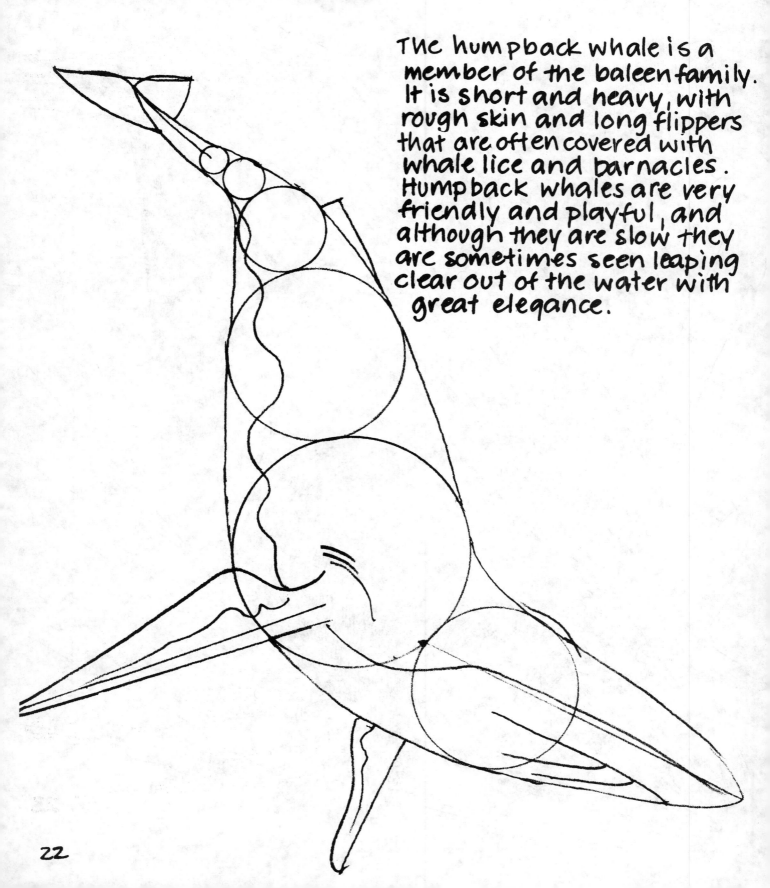

GRAY WHALE (<u>Eschrichtius robustus</u>)
North Atlantic, western Pacific, eastern Pacific

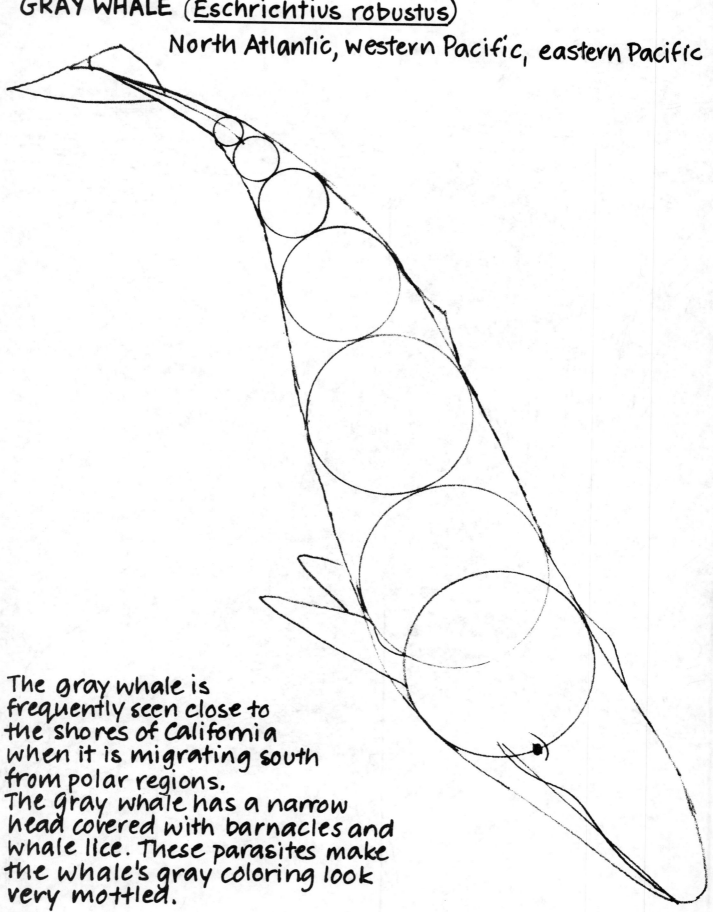

The gray whale is
frequently seen close to
the shores of California
when it is migrating south
from polar regions.
The gray whale has a narrow
head covered with barnacles and
whale lice. These parasites make
the whale's gray coloring look
very mottled.

24

BLUE WHALE (<u>Balaenoptera musculus</u>)

North Pacific, North Atlantic, and colder
waters of the Southern Hemisphere

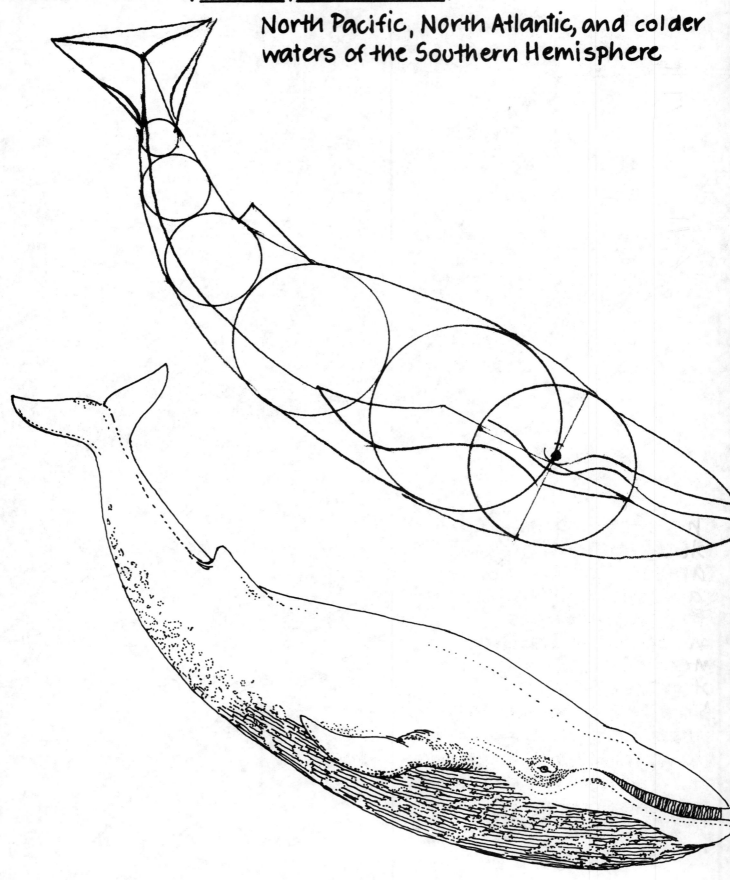

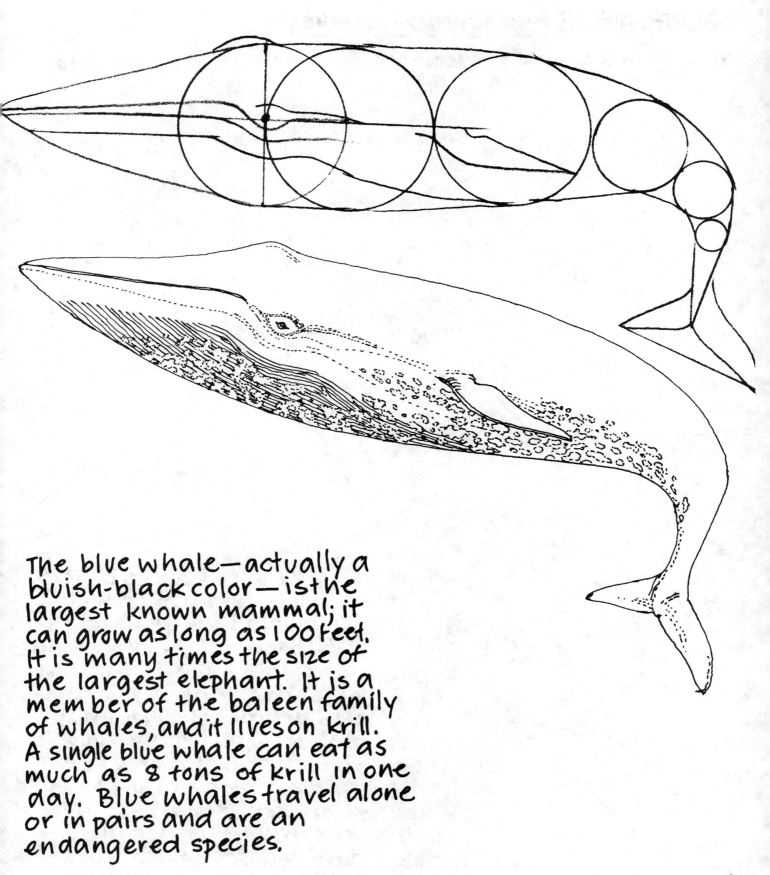

The blue whale—actually a
bluish-black color—is the
largest known mammal; it
can grow as long as 100 feet.
It is many times the size of
the largest elephant. It is a
member of the baleen family
of whales, and it lives on krill.
A single blue whale can eat as
much as 8 tons of krill in one
day. Blue whales travel alone
or in pairs and are an
endangered species.

SEI WHALE (<u>Balaenoptera borealis</u>)
Atlantic and Pacific oceans

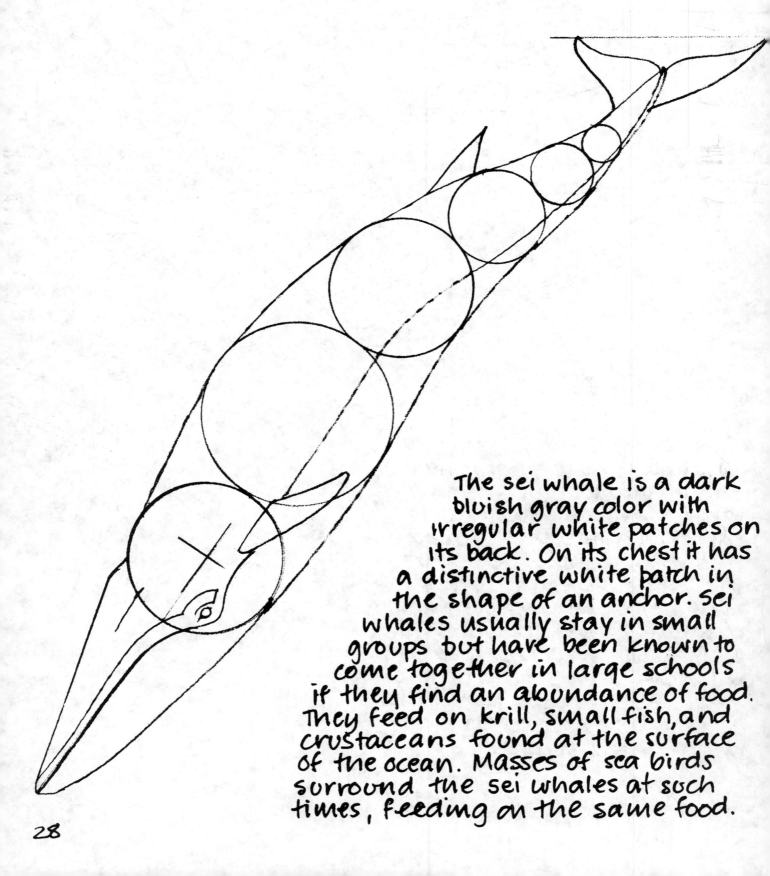

The sei whale is a dark bluish gray color with irregular white patches on its back. On its chest it has a distinctive white patch in the shape of an anchor. Sei whales usually stay in small groups but have been known to come together in large schools if they find an abundance of food. They feed on krill, small fish, and crustaceans found at the surface of the ocean. Masses of sea birds surround the sei whales at such times, feeding on the same food.

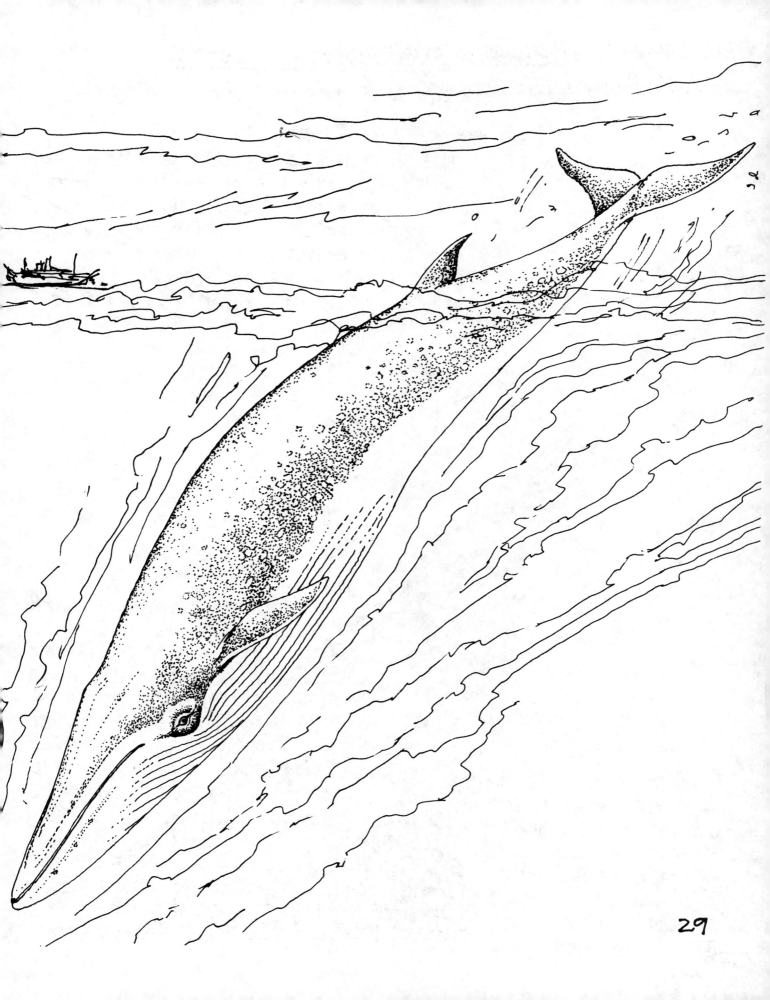

29

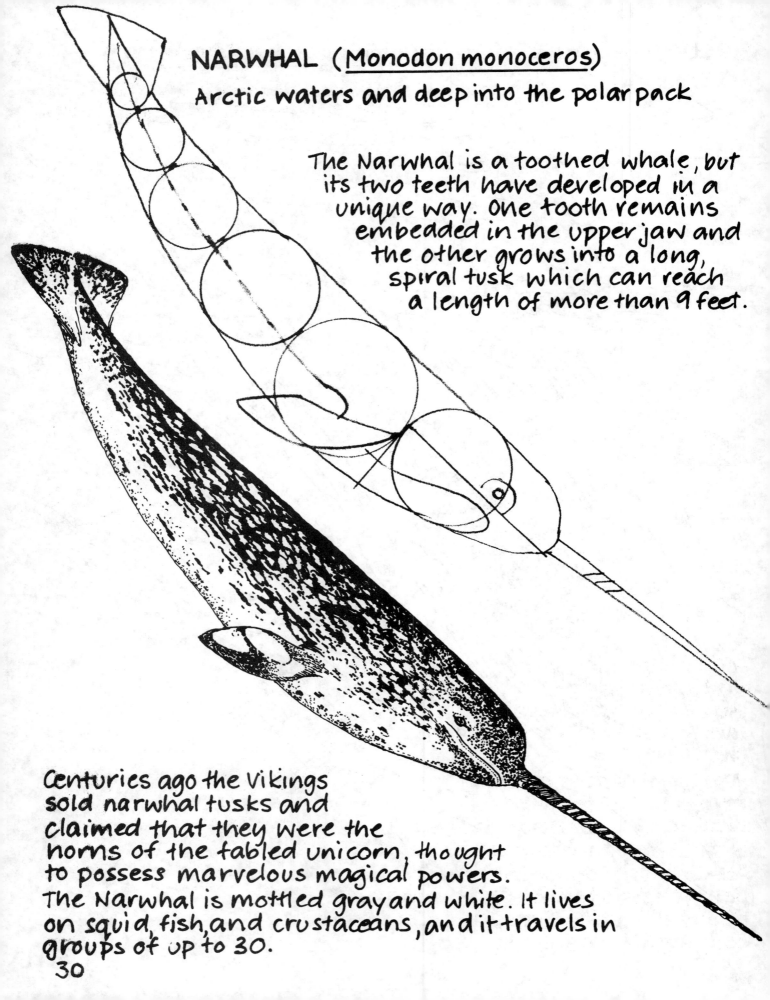

NARWHAL (<u>Monodon monoceros</u>)
Arctic waters and deep into the polar pack

The Narwhal is a toothed whale, but its two teeth have developed in a unique way. One tooth remains embedded in the upper jaw and the other grows into a long, spiral tusk which can reach a length of more than 9 feet.

Centuries ago the Vikings sold narwhal tusks and claimed that they were the horns of the fabled unicorn, thought to possess marvelous magical powers.
The Narwhal is mottled gray and white. It lives on squid, fish, and crustaceans, and it travels in groups of up to 30.

BELUGA or WHITE WHALE (<u>Delphinapterus leucas</u>)

Arctic and subarctic waters of Alaska, Canada, Greenland, and the U.S.S.R.

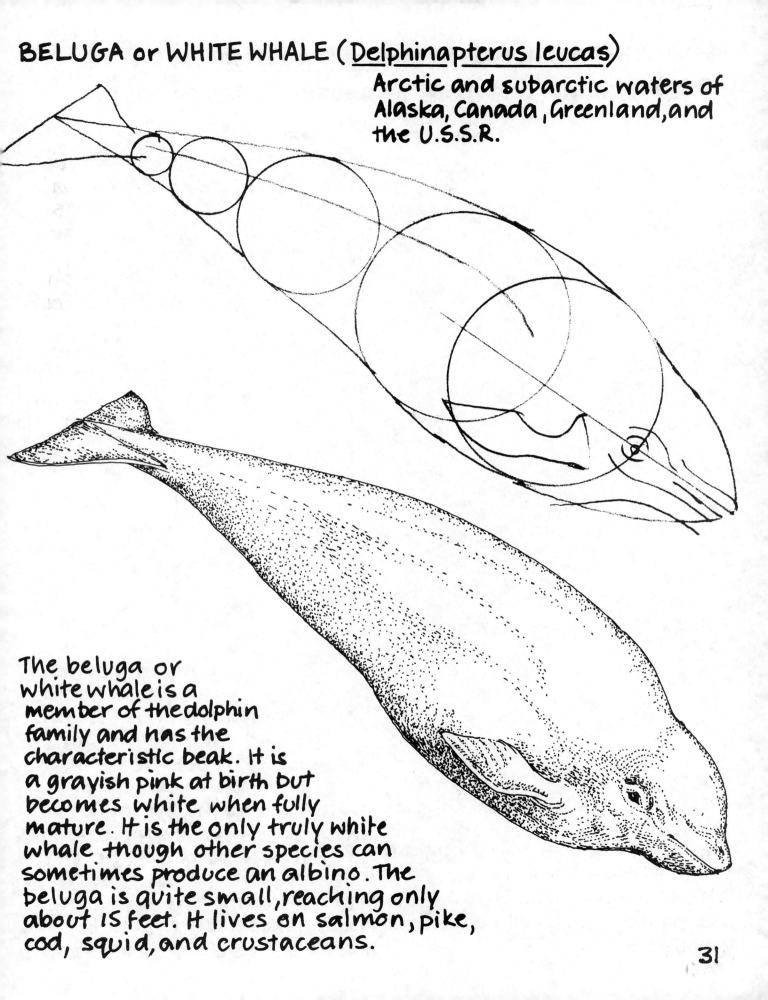

The beluga or white whale is a member of the dolphin family and has the characteristic beak. It is a grayish pink at birth but becomes white when fully mature. It is the only truly white whale though other species can sometimes produce an albino. The beluga is quite small, reaching only about 15 feet. It lives on salmon, pike, cod, squid, and crustaceans.

BOTTLENOSE WHALE (genus <u>Hyperoodon</u>)
North Atlantic and Mediterranean

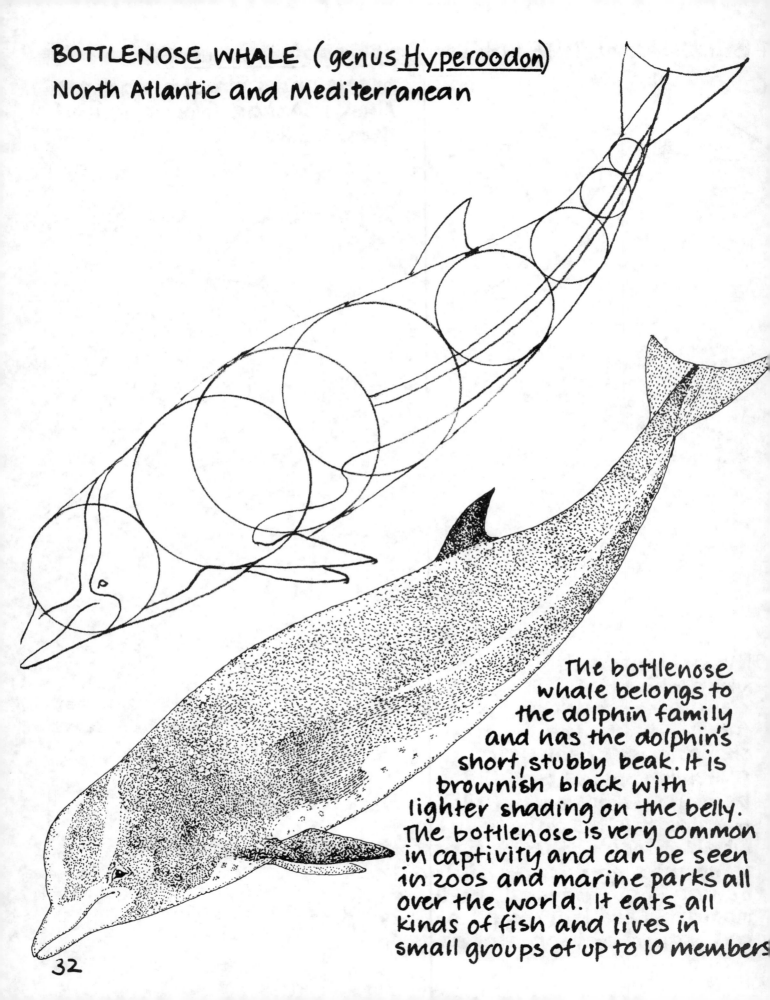

The bottlenose whale belongs to the dolphin family and has the dolphin's short, stubby beak. It is brownish black with lighter shading on the belly. The bottlenose is very common in captivity and can be seen in zoos and marine parks all over the world. It eats all kinds of fish and lives in small groups of up to 10 members.

FINBACK WHALE (<u>Balaenoptera physalus</u>)
Oceans throughout the world

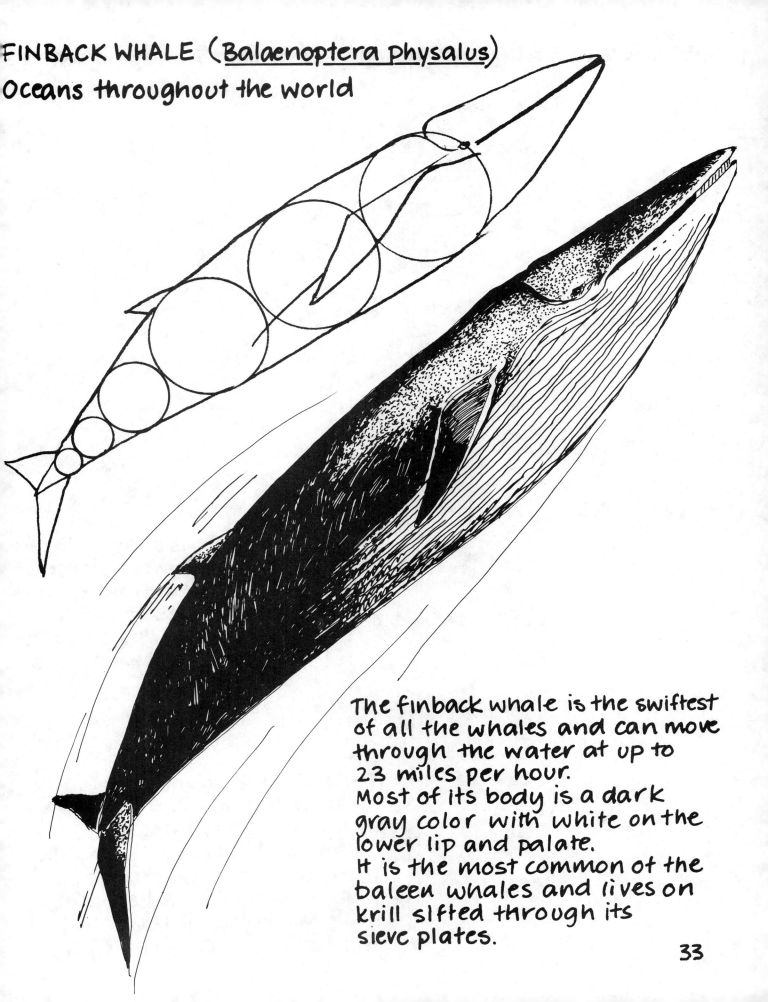

The finback whale is the swiftest of all the whales and can move through the water at up to 23 miles per hour.
Most of its body is a dark gray color with white on the lower lip and palate.
It is the most common of the baleen whales and lives on krill sifted through its sieve plates.

KILLER WHALE (<u>Orcinus orca</u>) Arctic and Antarctic waters

The killer whale is a large dolphin and is by far the most fierce of all the marine mammals. Killer whales travel in groups of up to 10 members.

They often attack in packs. Their prey includes seals, whales, and dolphins. Their shape is very easy to recognize, with a large upright dorsal fin. Killer whales have sharp, white markings on the belly and over the eye.

CUVIER'S BEAKED WHALE (<u>Ziphius cavirostris</u>)
All oceans of the world

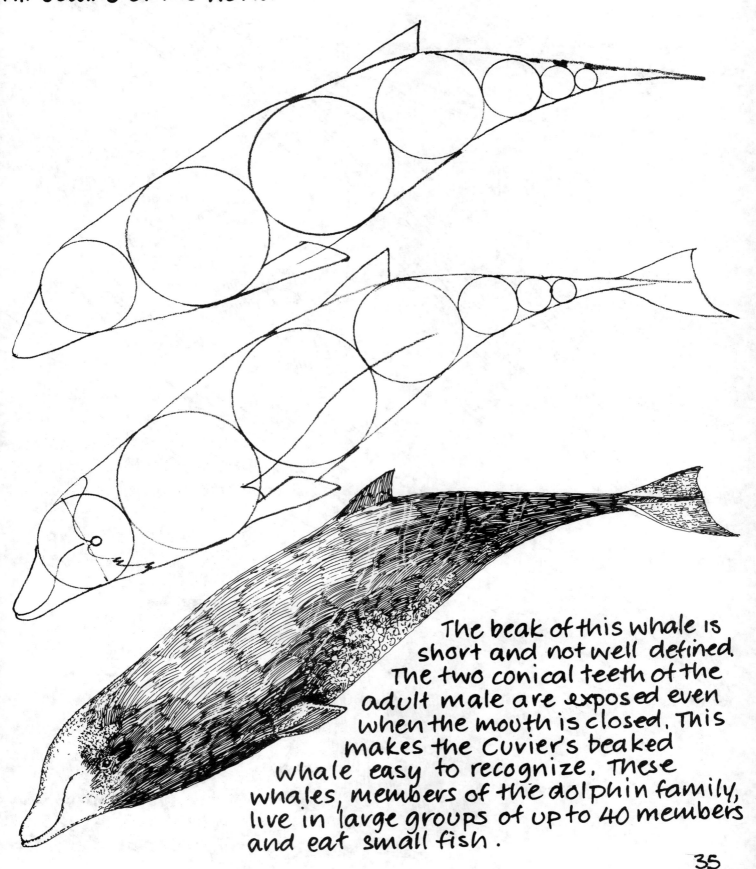

The beak of this whale is short and not well defined. The two conical teeth of the adult male are exposed even when the mouth is closed. This makes the Cuvier's beaked whale easy to recognize. These whales, members of the dolphin family, live in large groups of up to 40 members and eat small fish.

35

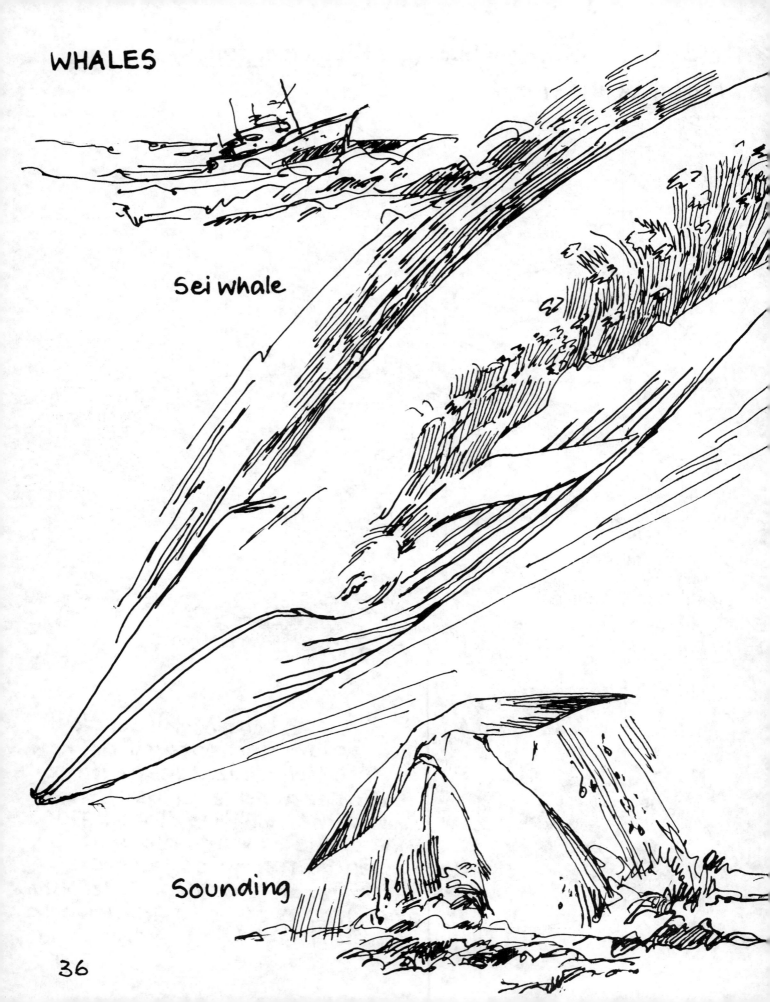

WHALES

Sei whale

Sounding

Spouting

Sperm whale

SKELETON AND BASIC SHAPE OF THE SHARK

The shark is not a mammal. Its ancestors are as ancient as the whale's, but the shark family ceased its evolution at a very early stage. The skeleton of the shark is made out of gristle or cartilage rather than bone. Gristle forms the mouth and a support and protection for the stomach.

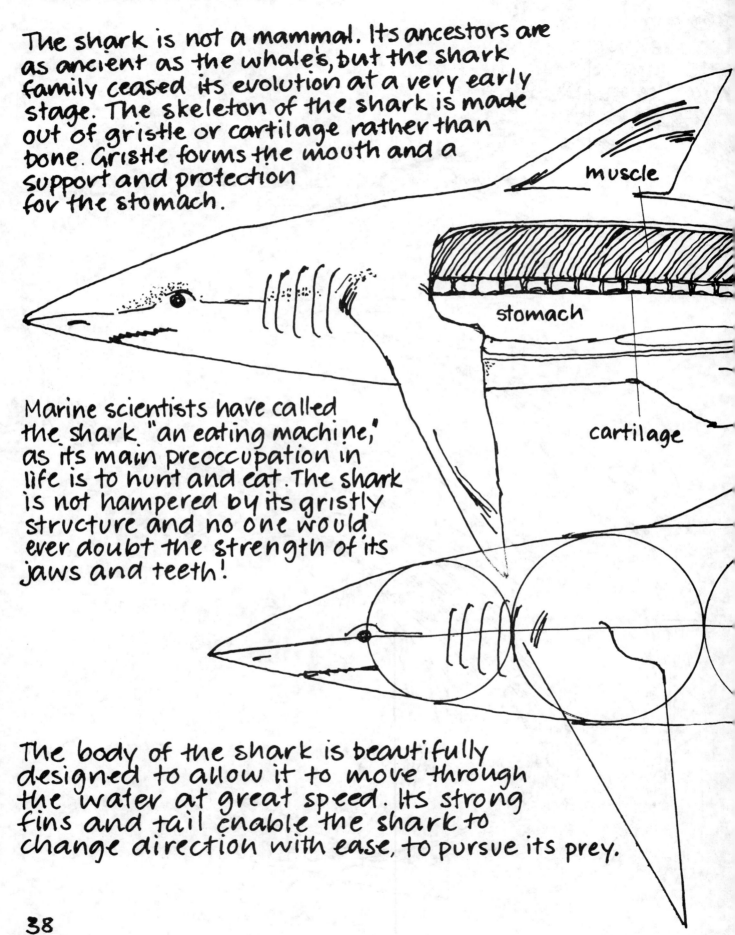

muscle

stomach

cartilage

Marine scientists have called the shark "an eating machine," as its main preoccupation in life is to hunt and eat. The shark is not hampered by its gristly structure and no one would ever doubt the strength of its jaws and teeth!

The body of the shark is beautifully designed to allow it to move through the water at great speed. Its strong fins and tail enable the shark to change direction with ease, to pursue its prey.

The shark does not have an air bladder, which enables fish to idle underwater. The shark must keep moving to be able to breathe.

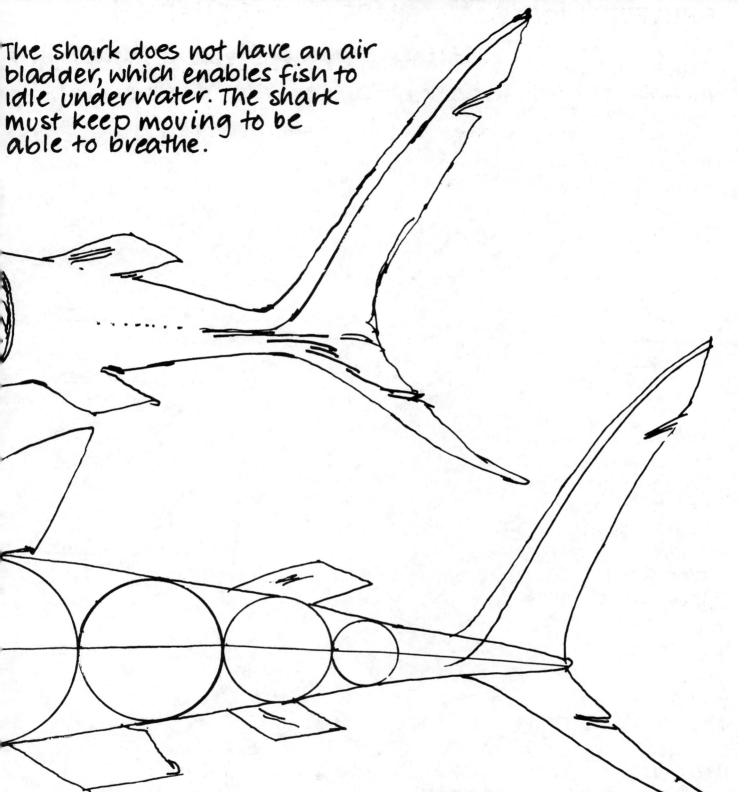

Sharks have few natural enemies and a reputation for brutal attacks on man. In fact, only very few sharks have been known to attack humans, and most prefer to hunt in deep waters away from the shore.

SWELL SHARK (Cephaloscyllium ventriosum)
Pacific ocean off Mexico and California

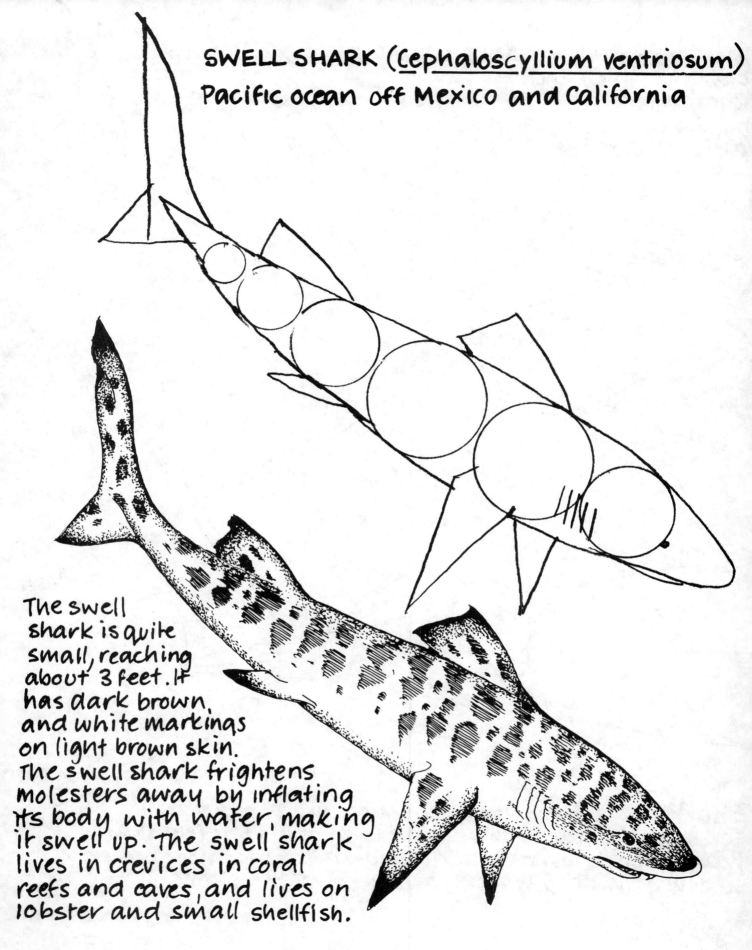

The swell shark is quite small, reaching about 3 feet. It has dark brown and white markings on light brown skin. The swell shark frightens molesters away by inflating its body with water, making it swell up. The swell shark lives in crevices in coral reefs and caves, and lives on lobster and small shellfish.

40

GRAY REEF SHARK (<u>Carcharhinus amblyrhynchos</u>)
Coastal waters of the tropics

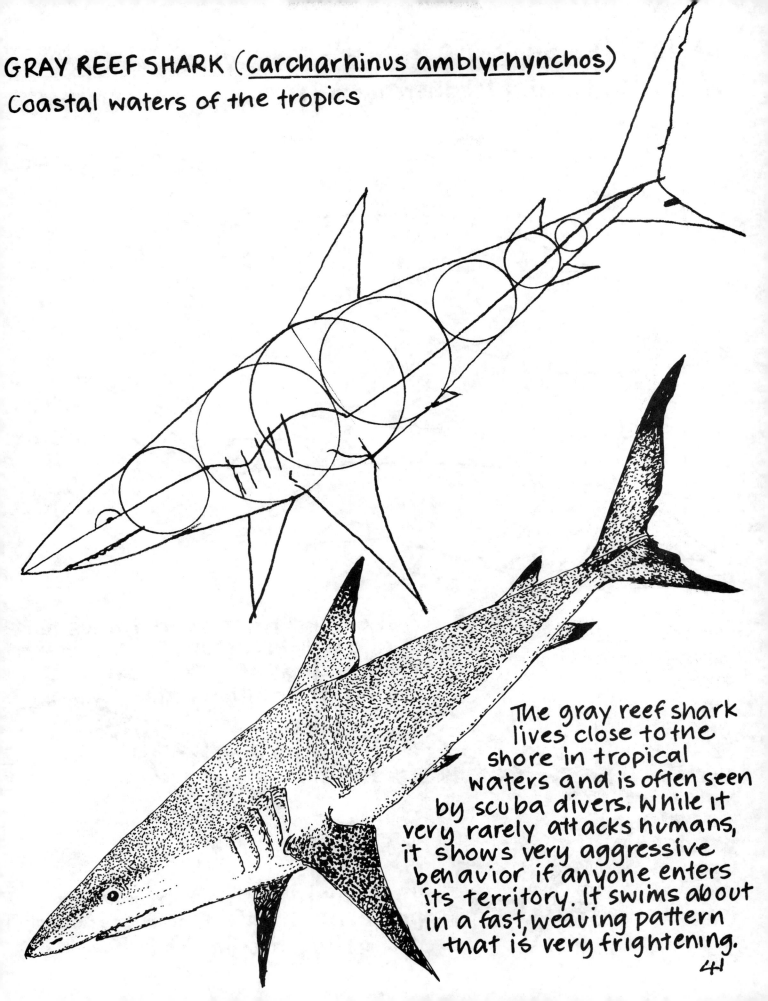

The gray reef shark lives close to the shore in tropical waters and is often seen by scuba divers. While it very rarely attacks humans, it shows very aggressive behavior if anyone enters its territory. It swims about in a fast, weaving pattern that is very frightening.

41

SAND TIGER SHARK (<u>Odontaspis taurus</u>)
West Atlantic and Mediterranean

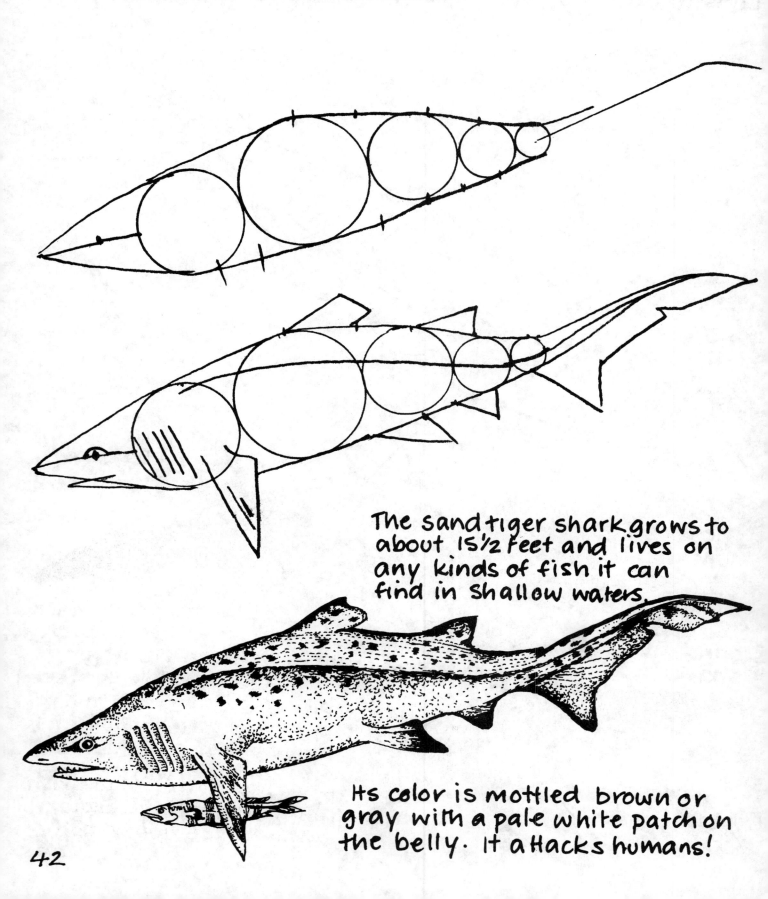

The sand tiger shark grows to about 15½ feet and lives on any kinds of fish it can find in shallow waters.

Its color is mottled brown or gray with a pale white patch on the belly. It attacks humans!

TIGER SHARK (Galeocerdo cuvieri)
Tropical and subtropical waters

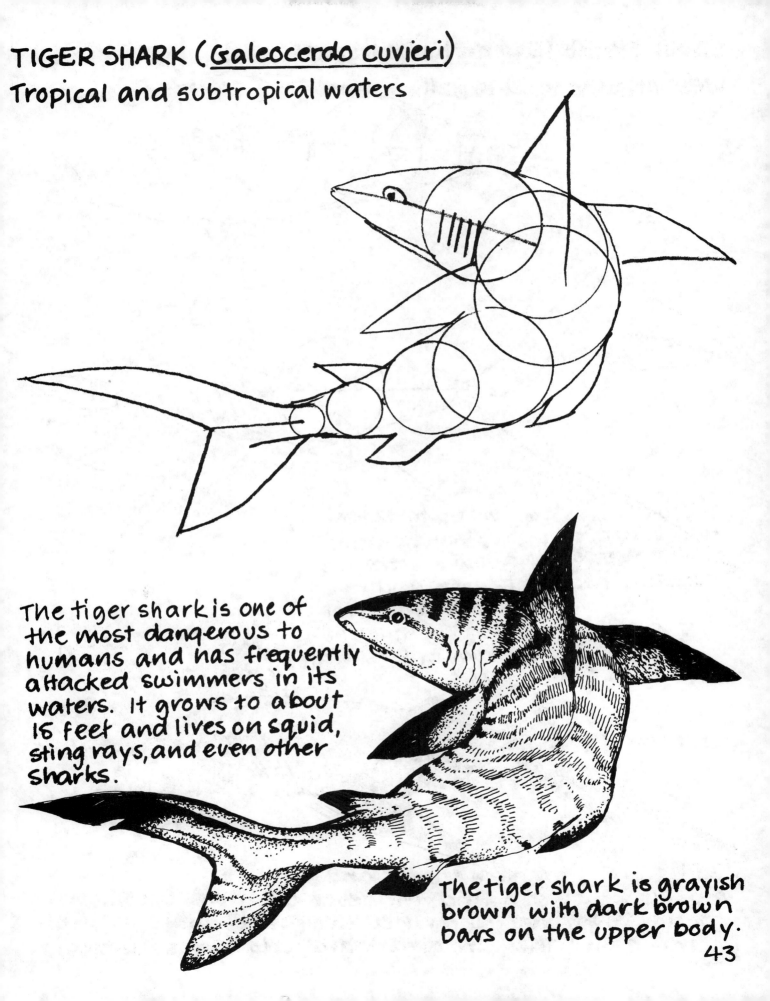

The tiger shark is one of the most dangerous to humans and has frequently attacked swimmers in its waters. It grows to about 18 feet and lives on squid, sting rays, and even other sharks.

The tiger shark is grayish brown with dark brown bars on the upper body.

43

BULL SHARK (<u>Carcharhinus leucas</u>)
North Atlantic to Brazil

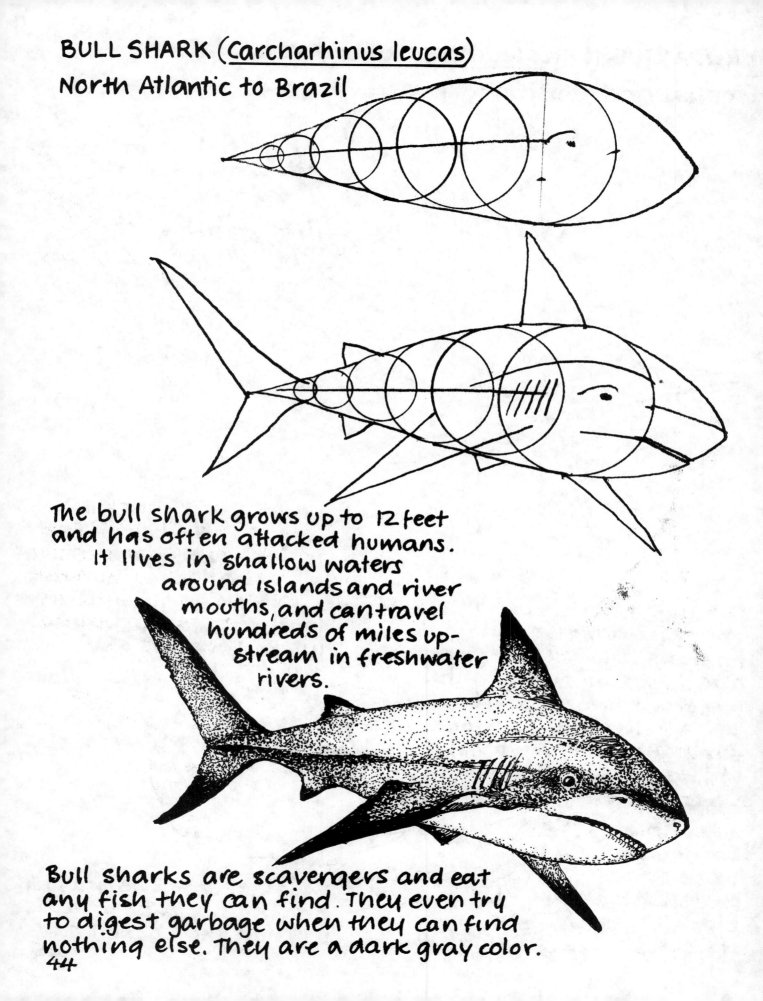

The bull shark grows up to 12 feet and has often attacked humans. It lives in shallow waters around islands and river mouths, and can travel hundreds of miles upstream in freshwater rivers.

Bull sharks are scavengers and eat any fish they can find. They even try to digest garbage when they can find nothing else. They are a dark gray color.

LEOPARD SHARK (<u>Triakis samifaciata</u>)
Eastern North Pacific

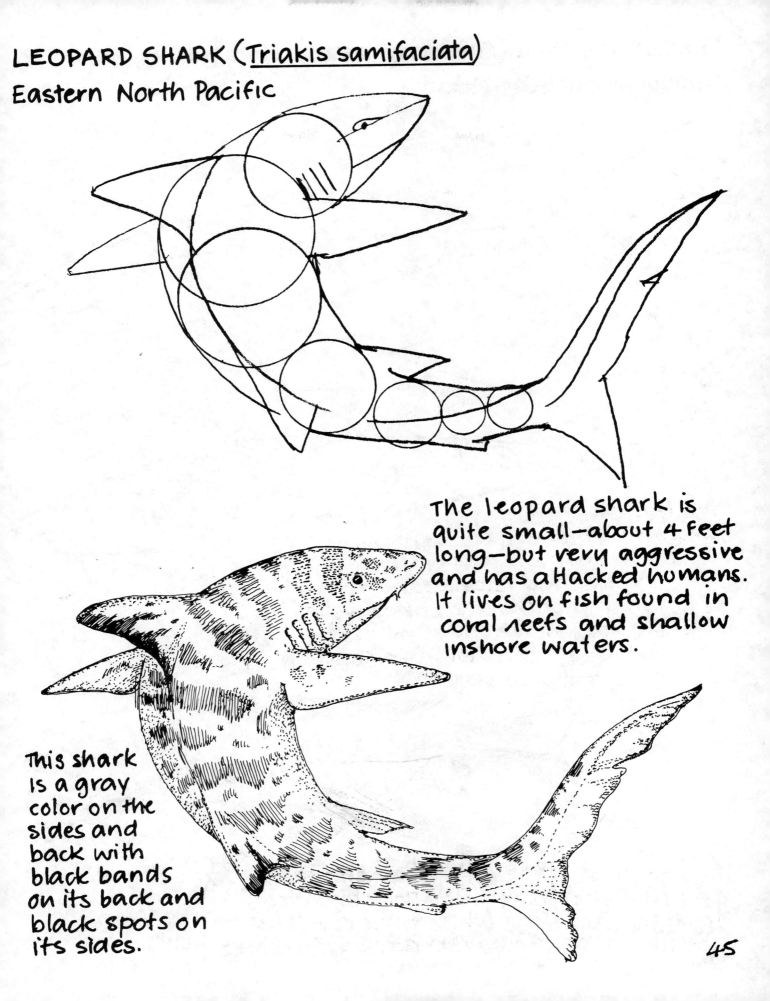

The leopard shark is quite small—about 4 feet long—but very aggressive and has aHacked humans. It lives on fish found in coral reefs and shallow inshore waters.

This shark is a gray color on the sides and back with black bands on its back and black spots on its sides.

45

BLACKTIP SHARK (<u>Carcharhinus maculipinnus</u>)
Throughout the Caribbean

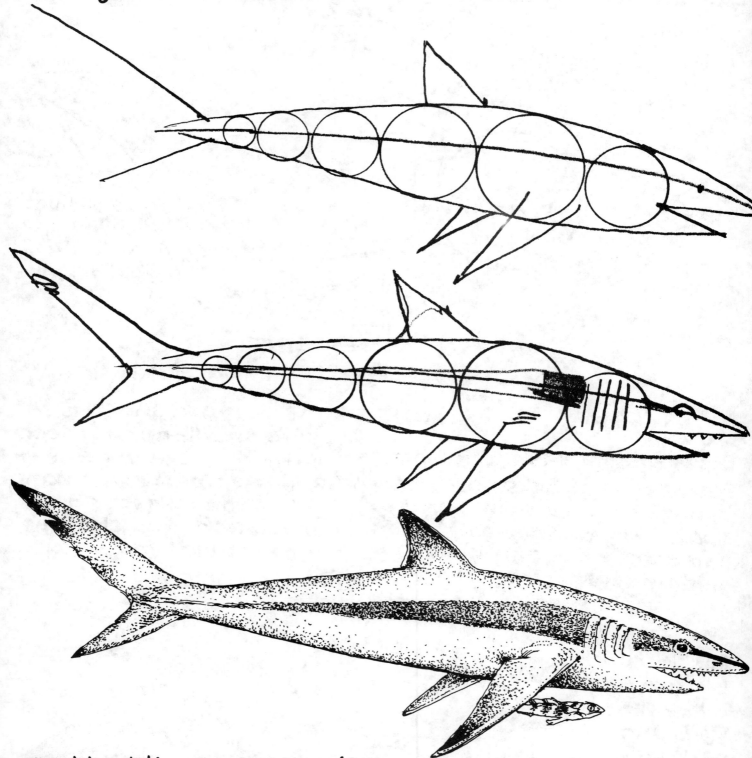

The blacktip shark takes its name from the black tips that edge its tail and fins. A black stripe also runs along its side from nose to tail. Blacktip sharks live on fish and have been suspected of attacking humans.

GREAT WHITE SHARK (Carcharodon carcharius)

Open oceans as well as coral reefs

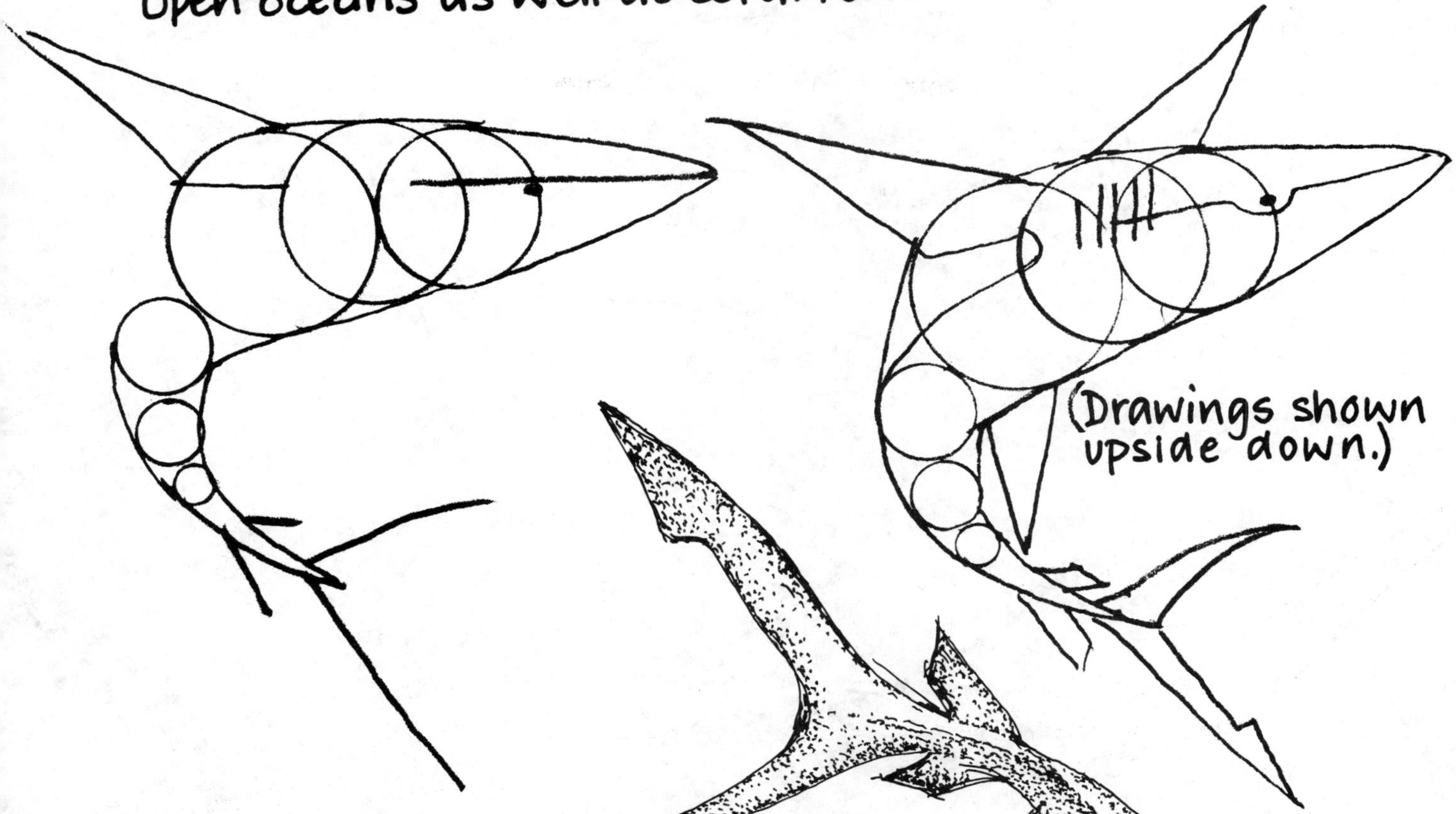

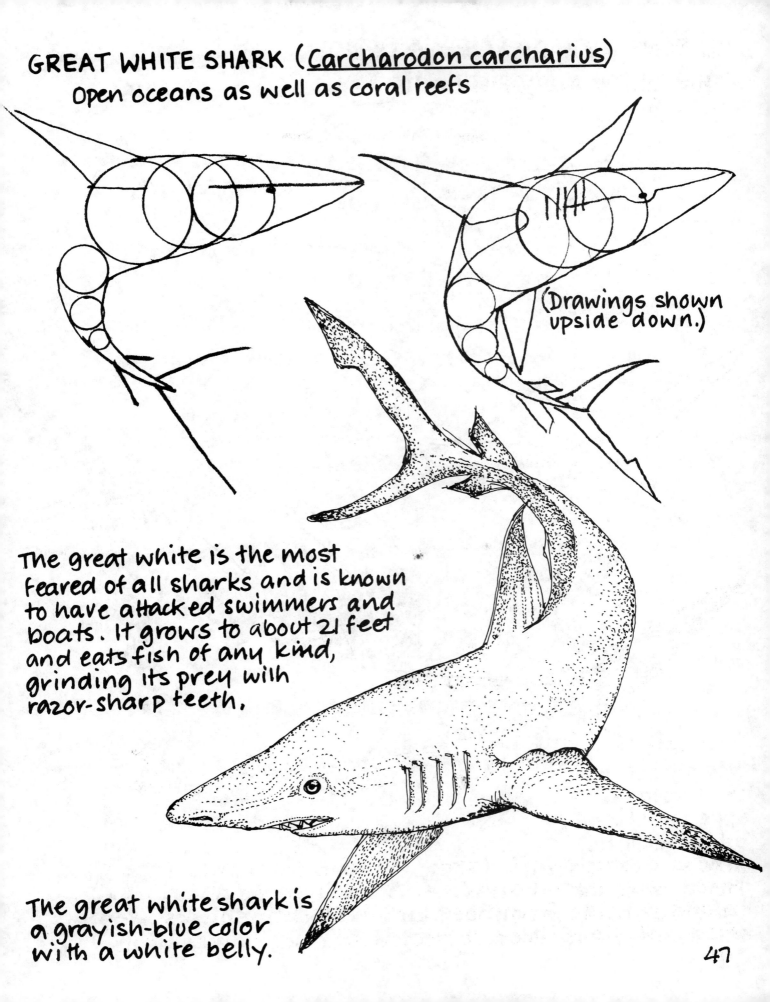

(Drawings shown upside down.)

The great white is the most feared of all sharks and is known to have attacked swimmers and boats. It grows to about 21 feet and eats fish of any kind, grinding its prey with razor-sharp teeth.

The great white shark is a grayish-blue color with a white belly.

THRESHER SHARK (<u>Alopias vulpinus</u>)
Tropical and subtropical waters

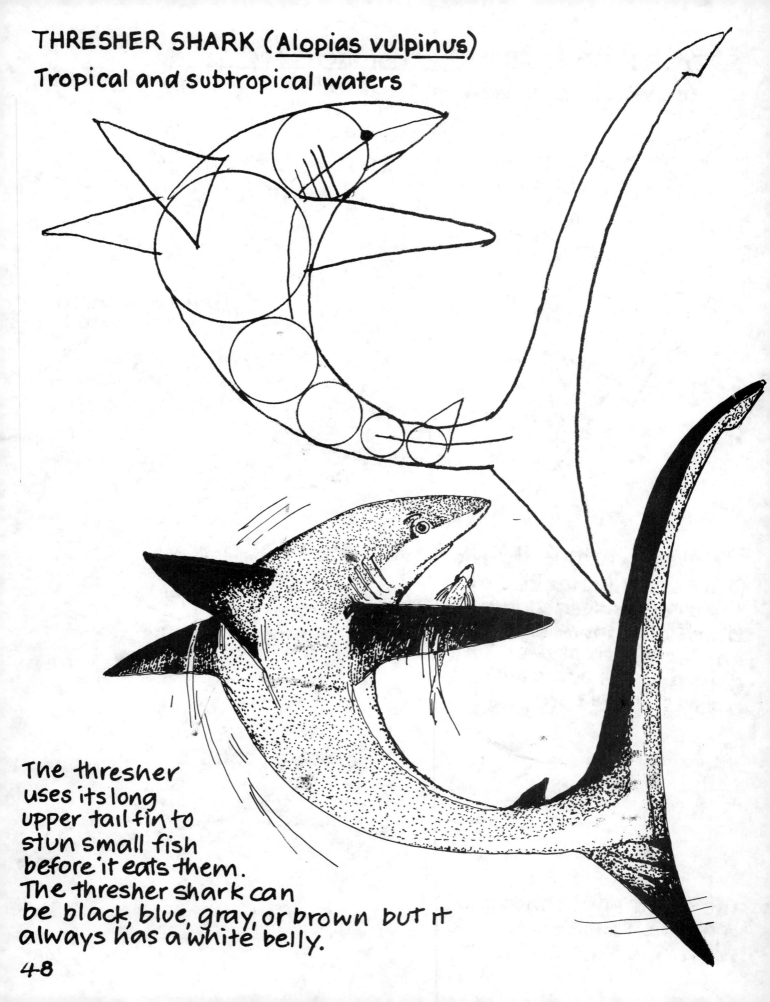

The thresher
uses its long
upper tail fin to
stun small fish
before it eats them.
The thresher shark can
be black, blue, gray, or brown but it
always has a white belly.

48

ZEBRA SHARK (<u>Stegostoma varium</u>)
Western Pacific and Indian Ocean

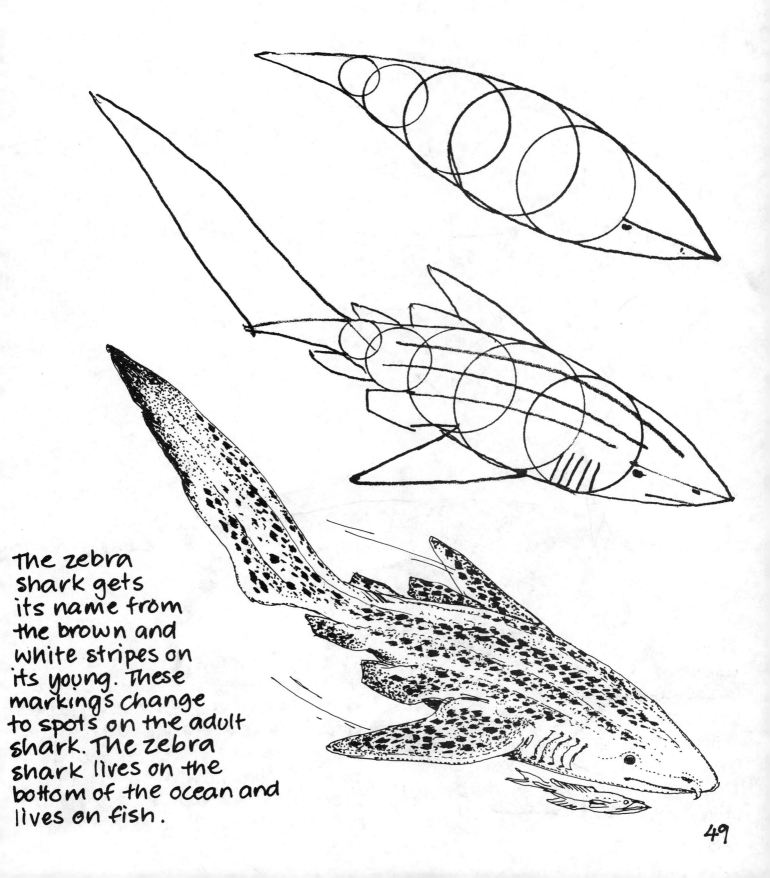

The zebra shark gets its name from the brown and white stripes on its young. These markings change to spots on the adult shark. The zebra shark lives on the bottom of the ocean and lives on fish.

GREAT HAMMERHEAD SHARK (Sphyrna mokarran)
Tropical waters of the world

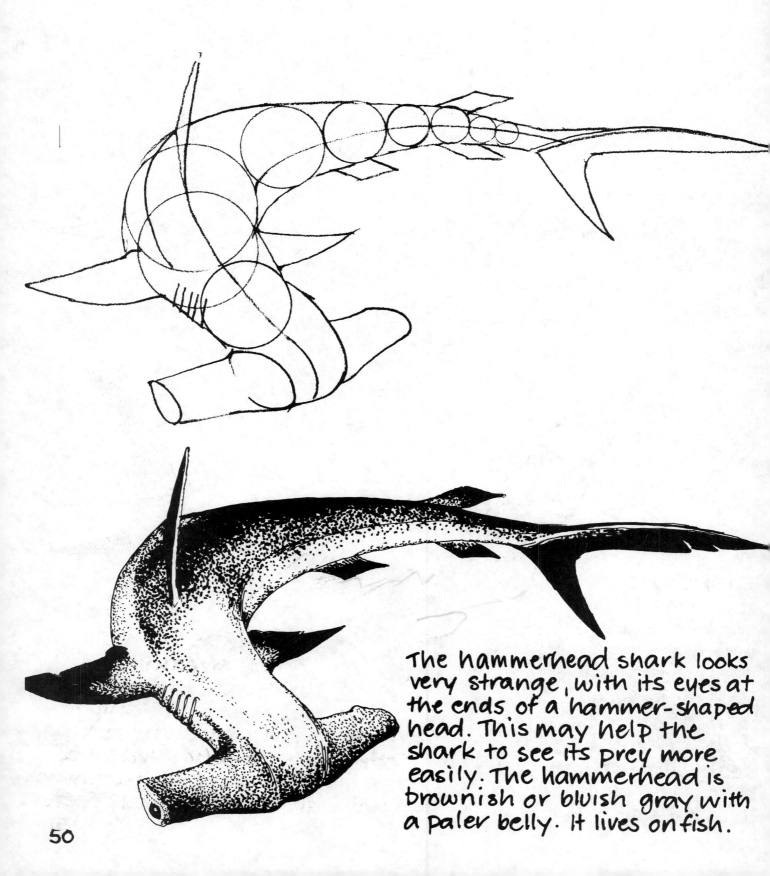

The hammerhead shark looks very strange, with its eyes at the ends of a hammer-shaped head. This may help the shark to see its prey more easily. The hammerhead is brownish or bluish gray with a paler belly. It lives on fish.

BLUE SHARK (_Prionace glauca_)
Temperate waters

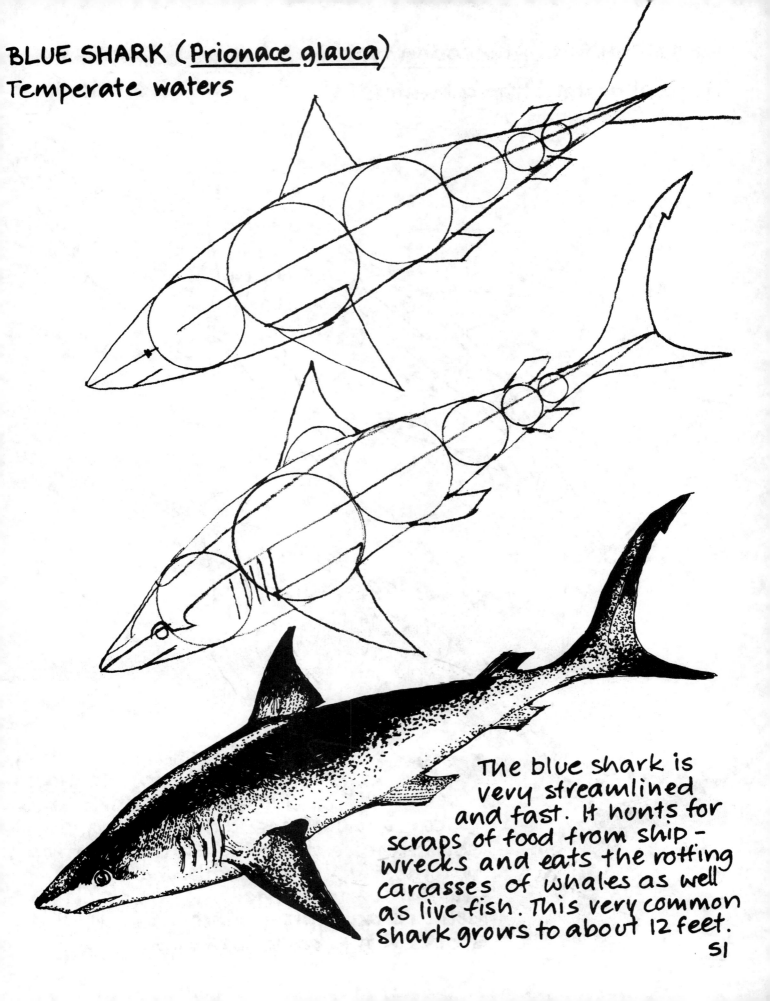

The blue shark is very streamlined and fast. It hunts for scraps of food from ship-wrecks and eats the rotting carcasses of whales as well as live fish. This very common shark grows to about 12 feet.

WHALE SHARK (<u>Rhincodon typus</u>)
Tropical and subtropical waters

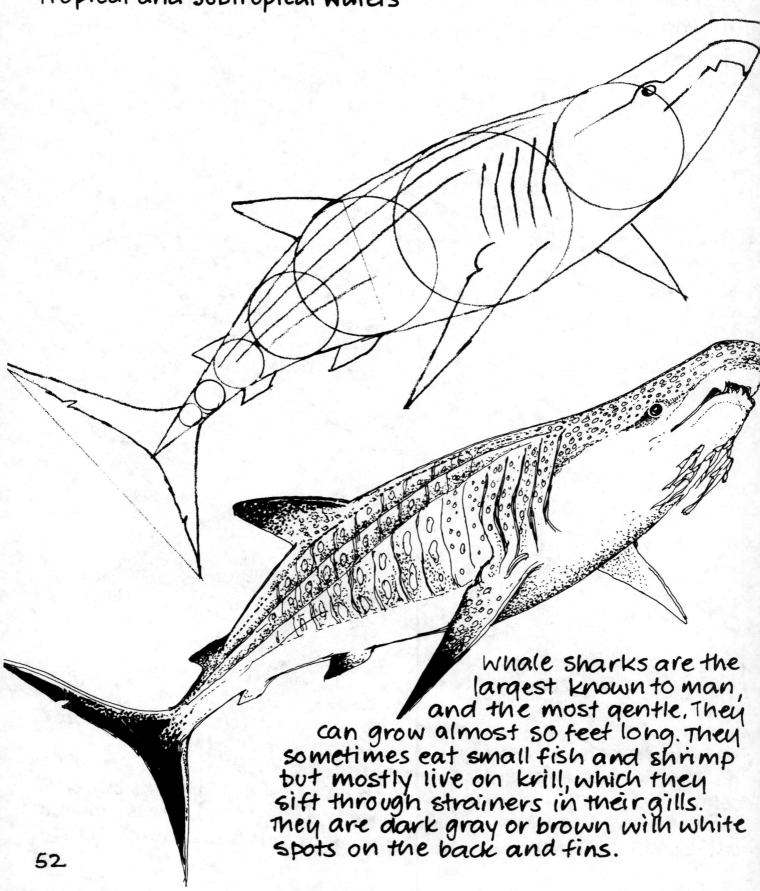

Whale sharks are the largest known to man, and the most gentle. They can grow almost 50 feet long. They sometimes eat small fish and shrimp but mostly live on krill, which they sift through strainers in their gills. They are dark gray or brown with white spots on the back and fins.

WHITETIP SHARK
(<u>Carcharhinus longimanus</u>)
All tropical and subtropical
waters

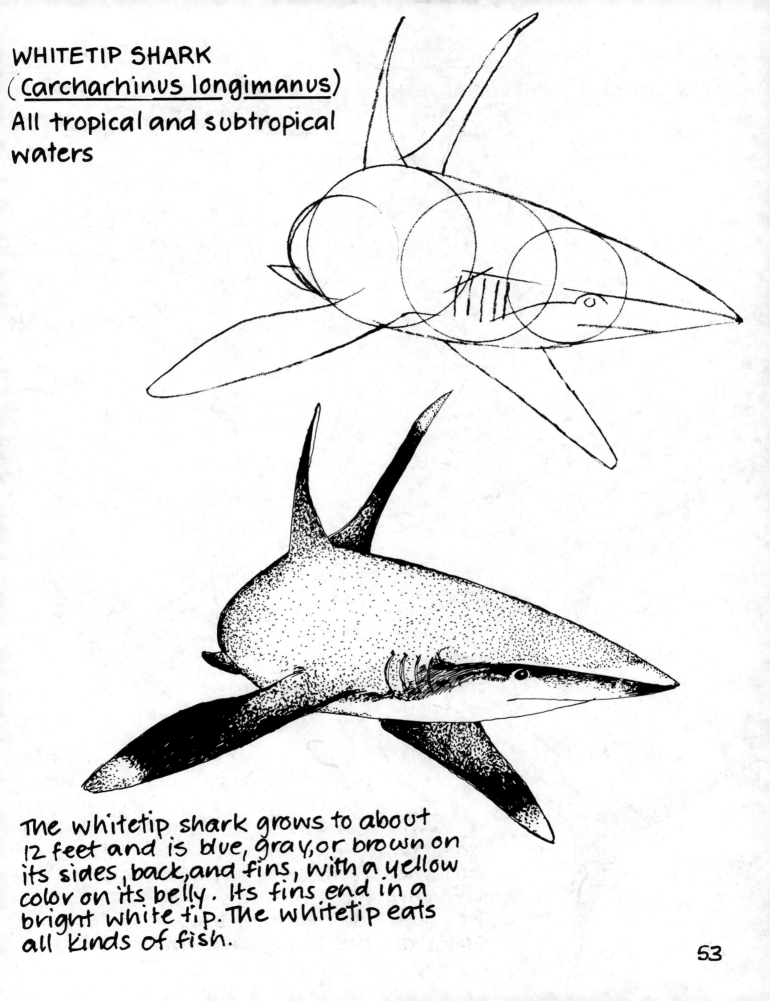

The whitetip shark grows to about
12 feet and is blue, gray, or brown on
its sides, back, and fins, with a yellow
color on its belly. Its fins end in a
bright white tip. The whitetip eats
all kinds of fish.

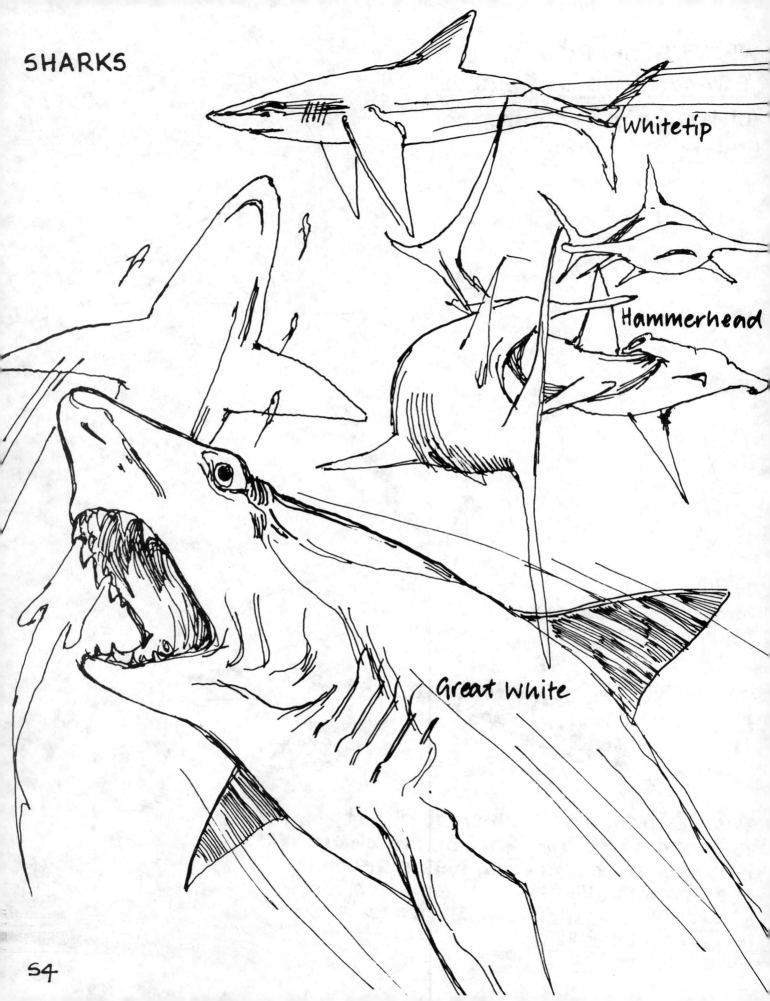

SHARKS

Whitetip

Hammerhead

Great white

54

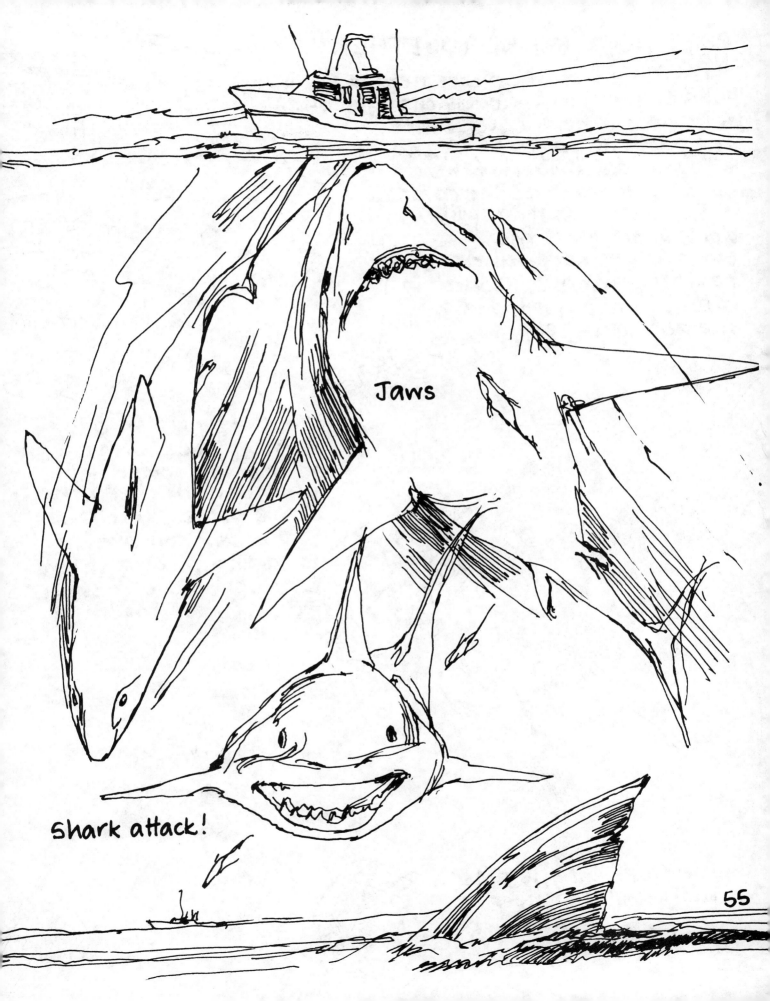

Jaws

Shark attack!

PUTTING A MODEL TOGETHER

You will find all the pieces needed for the whale and shark models on pages 59, 61, 63, and the back cover. Paste the parts on pages 59, 61, and 63 onto cardboard of the same thickness as the cover. If you don't want to spoil your book, trace the parts on the cover and paste these to cardboard also. Don't forget to mark the dots and letters.

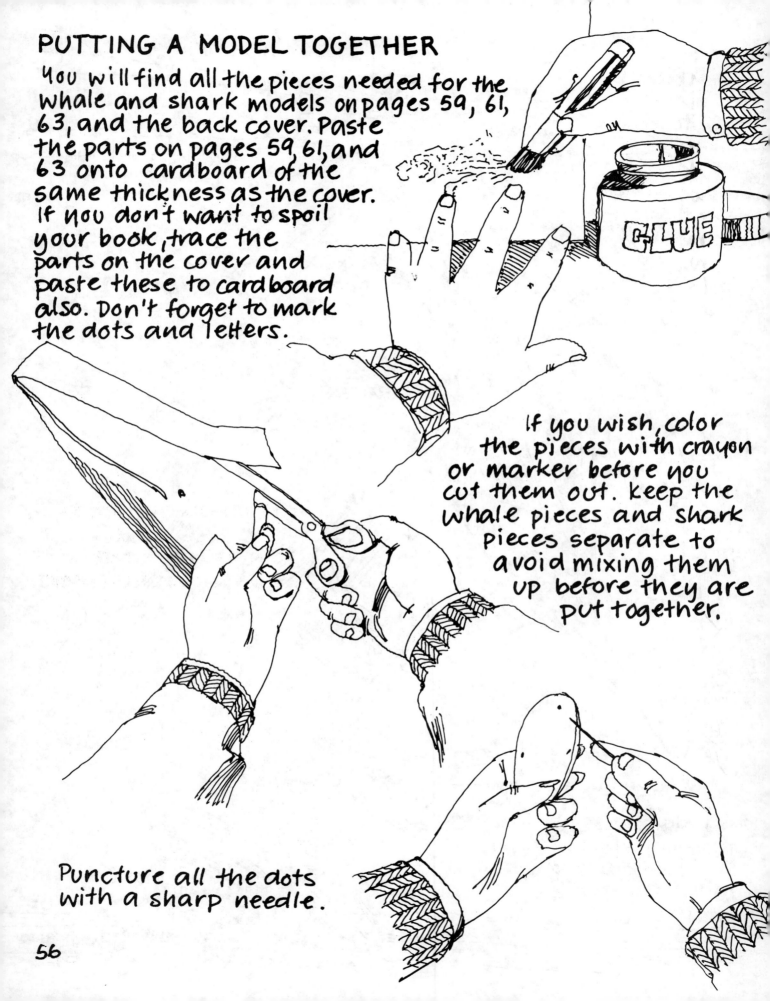

If you wish, color the pieces with crayon or marker before you cut them out. Keep the whale pieces and shark pieces separate to avoid mixing them up before they are put together.

Puncture all the dots with a sharp needle.

Assemble all the pieces you need to make a whale or a shark. Take care to choose the right parts. They are marked W1, W2, S1, and S2.

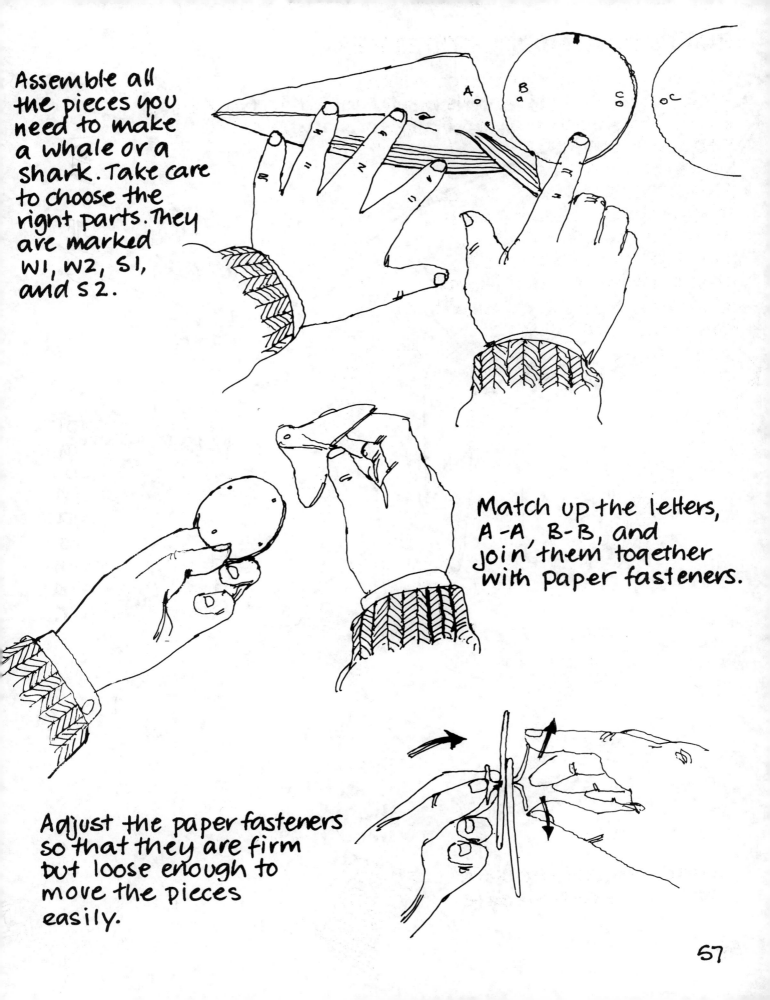

Match up the letters, A-A, B-B, and join them together with paper fasteners.

Adjust the paper fasteners so that they are firm but loose enough to move the pieces easily.

USING THE MODEL

Move the model into the pose you want to draw.

Hold the model in place on a sheet of paper.

Draw around the model, keeping the line as smooth as possible.

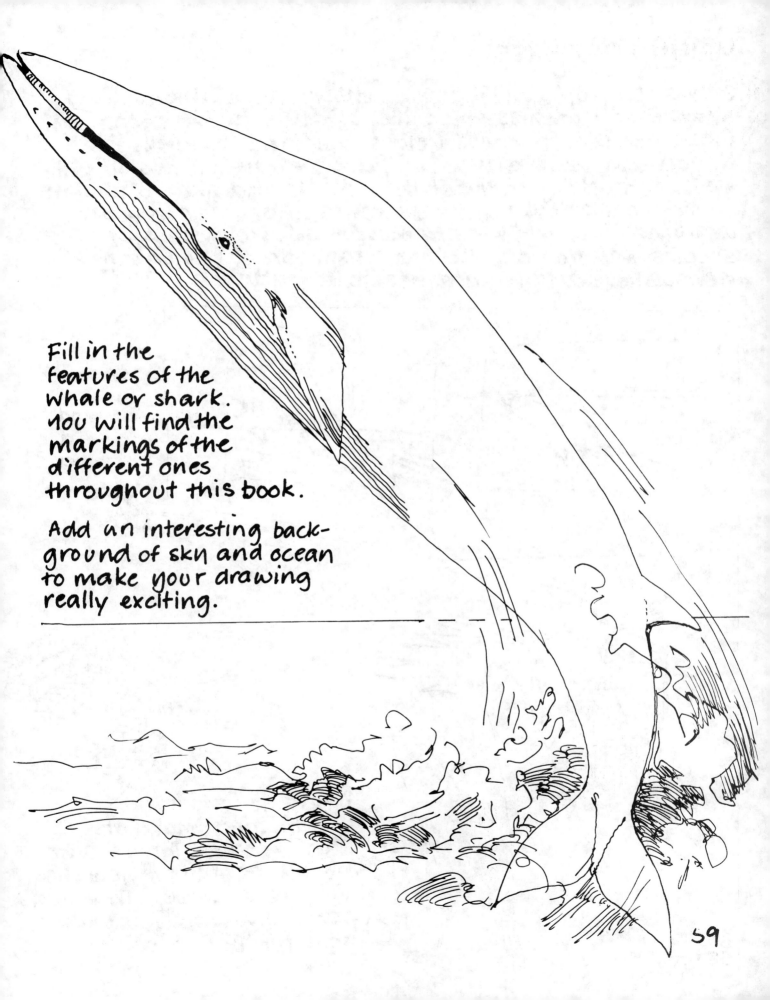

Fill in the
features of the
whale or shark.
You will find the
markings of the
different ones
throughout this book.

Add an interesting back-
ground of sky and ocean
to make your drawing
really exciting.

MAKING PICTURES

Only a few people will be lucky enough to be able to draw sharks and whales from life, but this needn't stop you from getting to know your subject really well.
If you can visit a marine park or aquarium you will be able to study some of the whales and sharks shown in this book. Make quick sketches to use later in your drawings. Natural-history museums have models of some species, and you can keep a scrapbook of photographs from newspapers and magazines to help you.

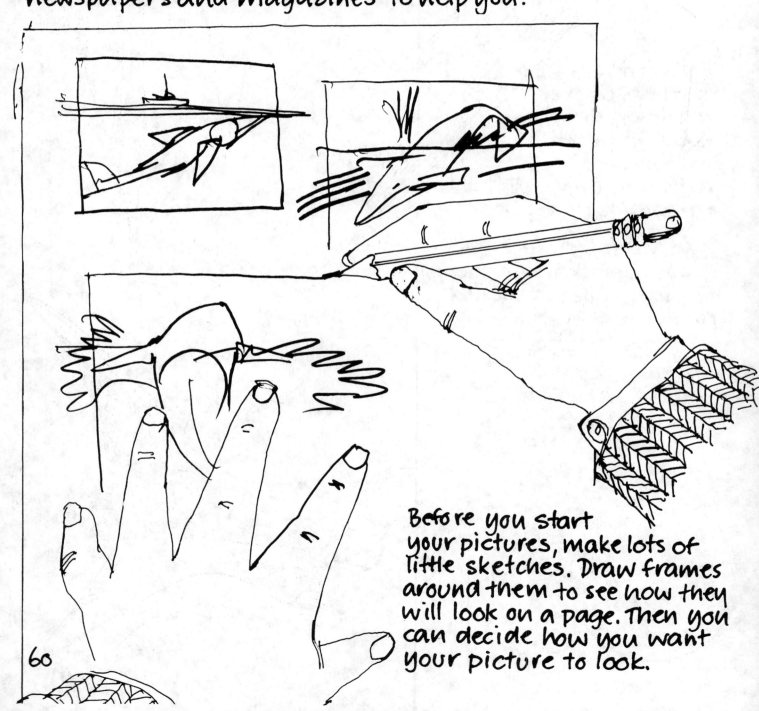

Before you start your pictures, make lots of little sketches. Draw frames around them to see how they will look on a page. Then you can decide how you want your picture to look.

PIECES FOR SHARK

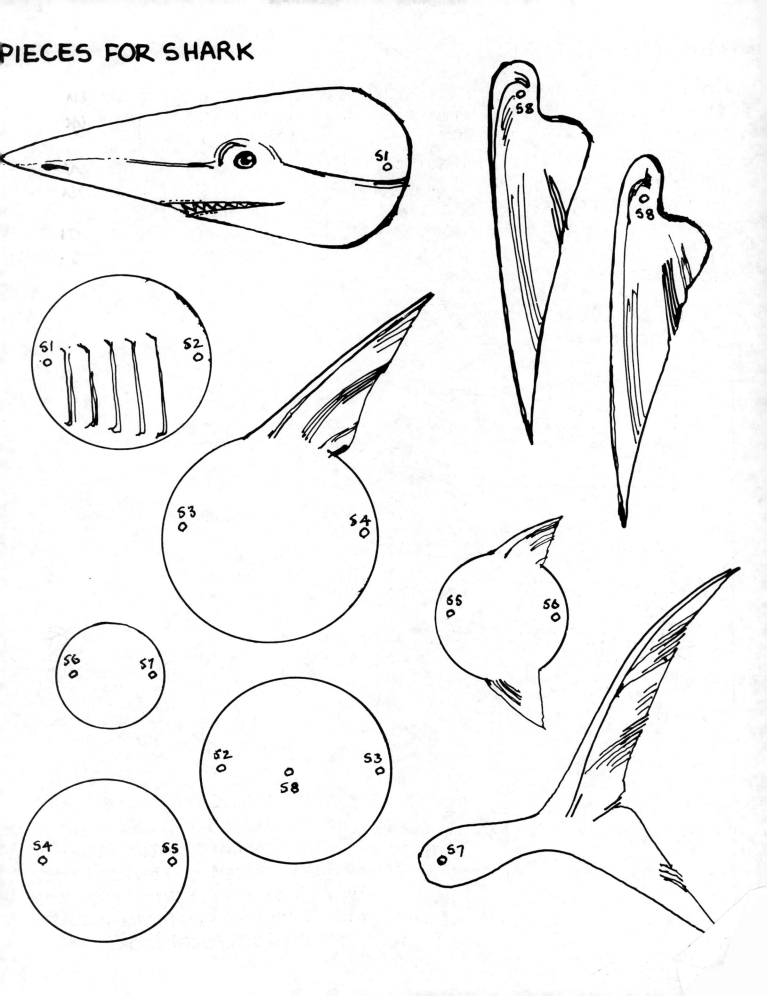

PIECES FOR SPERM WHALE (see back cover for sei whale)

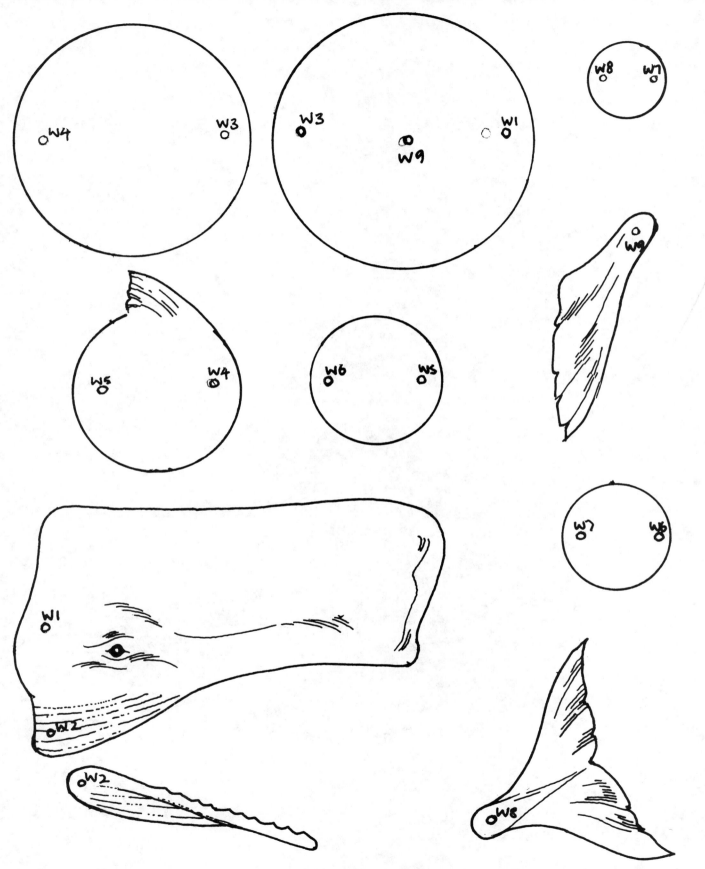

Have fun!